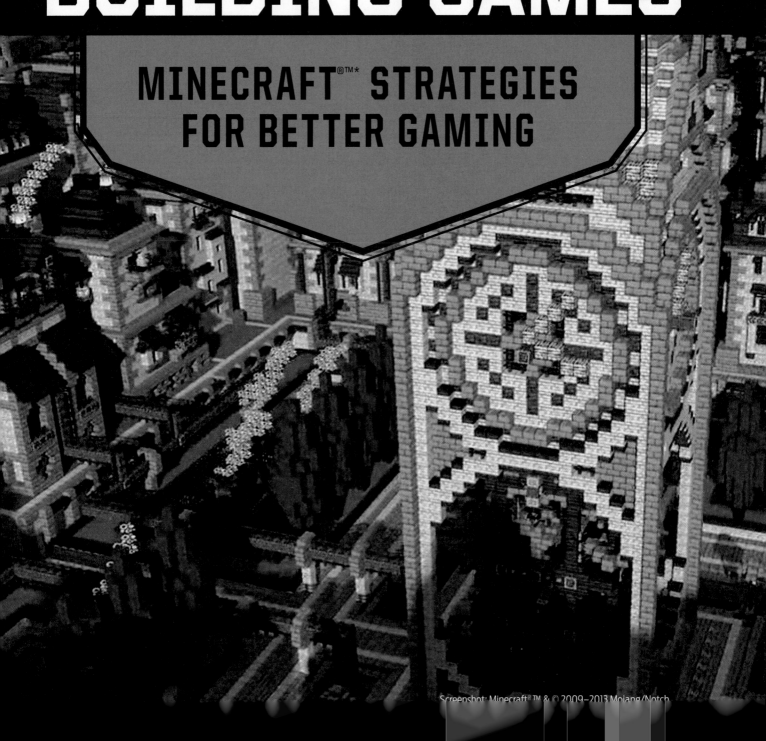

ESSENTIAL
BUILDING GAMES

MINECRAFT®™* STRATEGIES FOR BETTER GAMING

D1278993

This 2014 edition printed for Barnes & Noble, Inc.

Copyright © 2014 by Triumph Books LLC

Printed in U.S.A.
ISBN: 978-1-4351-5834-4

10 9 8 7 6 5 4 3

Contents

introduction
Here's Your Pickaxe & Helmet

If you've got this book in your hands, you've probably heard a bit about Minecraft. From its origins as a cult game with a small but dedicated following to a game played worldwide, Minecraft is pretty hard to miss these days. And there's a good reason for that.

Towers, castles and underground kingdoms—they're all possible in Minecraft

Put simply, Minecraft is one of the most inventive, creative and unique games ever created. Posing as a simple survival and world-building game, Minecraft fans have taken its unique system and caused it to blossom into something much more: a global cultural phenomenon.

In fact, Minecraft's genius has earned it so many fans all over the world, it's now considered one of the most successful games ever released for not one, but three major gaming systems (PC, Xbox 360 and smartphones). To put it in numerical terms: as of summer 2013, the game has sold over 28 *million* copies. That means that more people have purchased Minecraft than currently live in Australia.

With so many people taking the plunge into the crazy, block-filled world of Minecraft, it's no wonder you might be curious about the game. But like many before you, you might be asking yourself, "What is it about this low-resolution existence that people like so much?"

What is Minecraft?

Let's get this out of the way right off the bat: Minecraft is not like other games.

The basic premise of Minecraft is that you are a character who has spawned into a world that's entirely made up of materials, which you can harvest, and populated by creatures called mobs, which you can kill. Your immediate goal is this: survive.

There are animals and plants for food, and materials to build a shelter, but the world of Minecraft is not all out to help you. At night, hostile, dangerous mobs come out to try their best to kill you and maybe even wreck your home a bit.

Once you've secured your defenses against the dark, dark night, however, the resemblance to a typical video game ends.

Minecraft has little plot, the graphics are basic (though we think they're cool looking) and it rarely tells you what to do next. So why is Minecraft so popular?

More than Surviving
It's simple: Minecraft is whatever you want it to be. That might sound like exaggeration, but it really isn't. Everything you see in the world of Minecraft can be changed, from knocking down a tall mountain, to drying up a lake to building enormous structures that tower into the sky anywhere you like.

This is possible because everything in the environment of Minecraft is created by blocks, each of which is made up of a resource such as Stone or Wood. These blocks can be removed by "breaking" them, and you can then either use them to build the world the way you'd like, or you can turn them into even more materials and items. All it takes is a little exploring, and you can find the resources to create just about anything.

Explore, Explore and Explore Further
And Minecraft does not shirk or mess about when it comes to giving you plenty to explore. One of the master strokes of this modern classic game is that it uses complex algorithms to create massively diverse and unique worlds to explore every time you load it.

There are endless deserts populated by thriving villages and cut through with winding rivers. There are towering snowy mountains that cast shadows over sweeping plains dotted with flowers, lava fields and cave entrances. There are even multiple dimensions and an underground filled with ruins and adventures that will take you dozens of hours to fully explore, if you can survive the creatures that dwell there.

The Real Reason Minecraft is Great
In the end though, there's one reason Minecraft has cemented its status as a truly great game, and that's this: Minecraft is only limited by your imagination.

If you can think of it, you can build it or make it happen. That is, if you know how the game works.

What You'll Find in this Guide
We've put this guide together to help you with that "knowledge of the game" part of things. We want you to be the best Minecrafter you can be, and it's a time-honored Minecraft tradition for veteran players to pass down their knowledge to newcomers. Here you'll find everything you need to get started and begin your first monumental creation, but don't get us wrong, this guide isn't just for the noobs.

Minecrafter is also full of advanced info, exclusive strategies and tips and tricks that even the best pros will find useful. Within you'll come across detailed breakdowns of all the mobs, materials and menus, not to mention some of the most useful Minecraft inventions and farming/mining techniques.

Let's Build
Now, with the goal of surviving the dark night in order to bring staggering creations of beauty and wonder into the digital world, pick up your phone, mouse or Xbox controller, crack open this book and start up a fresh world of Minecraft.

It's time to build.

Note: this guide is written to be useful to all Minecrafters regardless of platform, but we have chosen the Xbox 360 version as our standard.

the phenomenon

"Now wait a second," you say, "I thought we were gonna build." Well, we are, and you can get to it right now by skipping ahead a bit if you're impatient! But, if you're interested in the background of this mind-bending game of imagination and blocks and Zombie Pigmen you're about to undertake, here's a bit of the story of how Minecraft came to be the gaming behemoth that it is. And oddly enough, it actually starts with three entirely different games.

Want to build a castle?

What about a pirate ship? Minecraft is all about that.

Rising From the Sandbox

Minecraft is what is known as a "sandbox" game. Sandbox means that the world of the game is entirely open and can be manipulated by the player. Instead of having a plot and gameplay that everyone experiences in basically the same way, sandbox games give the player some tools to change the world they see, and then they let that player decide what to do for him or herself.

Notch and His Three Inspirations

Minecraft might well be the best received and most well-known sandbox game made yet, but it was far from the first. In fact, the story of Minecraft's creation is the story of Swedish video game designer named Markus Alexej Persson and his love for three influential sandbox video games: 1997's *Dungeon Keeper*, a cult indie game called *Infiniminer* and a title with almost no graphics to speak of but an incredibly complex world, *Dwarf Fortress*.

While he worked away as a programmer at photo-sharing company Jalbum, Persson (soon to be called "Notch" by his fans) was enthralled with the idea of making a game that combined the elements of his three inspirations. Notch had been involved with the gaming world for a long time, having written his first game at the age of 8, not to mention working as a game designer and competing in game creation tournaments for many years. However, it was when Notch hit upon the idea of combining the styles of *Dwarf Fortress, Infiniminer* and *Dungeon Keeper* that his career as a gaming titan was to take off.

Combining the Influences

What Notch did was pretty darn close to genius: he pulled the focus on building and fantasy from *Dungeon Keeper;* the RPG elements, resource collecting and focus on memorable graphics over cutting-edge from *Dwarf Fortress;* and the block-by-block building innovation of *Infiniminer* and he combined them all into one game: an open-world, RPG fantasy that allowed players to destroy and build anything they wanted.

The Path to Glory

Of course, it didn't all happen overnight. Notch kept his job at Jalbum while working on Minecraft in his spare time, and the original game is a far cry from what you get now when you play it on your Xbox. At first, all you could do was build, there was little in the way of block-types and no creatures. As Notch continued to add elements, the game began to take shape and more and more players joined in the fun. YouTube and other Internet outlets spread the word like a wildfire across the web, and soon enough, there was a small but passionate fan base for the game.

Taking it Public

When people first started seriously playing Minecraft around 2009, it wasn't considered even remotely finished yet, but it was still such an engaging game that Notch was able to do quite well selling access to the pre-release version. Players who purchased it back then were guaranteed that they'd never have to pay for later versions (something which has stayed true to this day), and this combined with the low price to make it an instant underground classic. Within almost no time, people were creating things in Minecraft that the developers never dreamed of, not to mention modding the game more thoroughly than perhaps any other in video game history. Soon, though, the hardcore gamers would welcome millions of new players from the mainstream into their flocks, as the official version was released.

Minecraft Goes Big

The official release for the game came in 2011, and that's when things really took off. After only a month, the newly formed Mojang video game company, headed by Notch, had made 1 million sales of Minecraft. People thought this was insane for such an odd game from a new company, but that was just the beginning. Within a year, Minecraft had become the 6th best-selling PC game of all time with 5.3 million copies, more even than the beloved *Half-Life*. Again, people thought the trend had hit its peak, but no. In 2012, the Xbox 360 and Pocket Edition versions were released, shattering records and putting the game on the top sales lists for those two platforms as well.

The Sky's the Limit

Now, Minecraft has sold more than 28 million copies, putting it in the ranks with *Super Mario Brothers* and *Tetris* as one of the absolute success stories from the video gaming universe. Even the worlds of art and high-brow media have taken notice, with the Museum of Modern Art including Minecraft as one of just a few video games displayed within its hallowed halls, and with *Time* magazine including Notch and fellow creator Jeb as two of their 100 most influential people in the world for 2013.

The people have spoken: there's no doubt that it's a Minecraft world out there these days, and now you, reader, can join in those 28 million+ players and become part of a global phenomenon as it's happening. You've already shown you're ready by picking up this guide, so fire up that controller and sit yourself down someplace comfy. It's time you become one of us, Minecrafter.

getting started

So here you are, you've taken the plunge and bought Minecraft. You're staring at that menu screen, and you're ready to dive into this crazy world you've heard so much about.

Now, you could start up a new world and try and wing it, but trust us, that path leads to darkness (literally), frustration and, yes, death. Minecraft is a game that's at once very simple on the surface and incredibly complex underneath, and what you do when you first start out can make a huge difference in your success at crafting the world you want. That, plus it's really not much fun to die in the dark from your fourth Creeper attack in a row and lose all of your gear over and over.

To get the most out of Minecraft, you'll have a much better and less death-filled time if you know a few things about the game before jumping right in.

You're seconds from your first game of Minecraft

the menus

It only takes the push of a few buttons to start up a new Minecraft world, but the good folks at Mojang packed the Minecraft menus full of options that can make a big difference in your overall experience. Of particular importance are the "Help & Options" area and, of course, the "Play Game" button.

Help & Options

The title says it all—this is where you want to go to find everything from audio and visual settings to new skins for your avatar and mini-guides on how to deal with certain aspects of the game. Much of this can be accessed in-game, so it's not entirely necessary that you look through this or tweak it in any way until you've played a little, but it's good to know that it's there ahead of time.

Play Game

This is where the magic happens. The "Play Game" button is what kicks off your Minecraft experience, whether it's starting a new world with "Create New World," trying out the "Tutorial" or getting back into one of the games you've already begun. As you'll see, when you open the "Play Game" menu for the first time, you only have the option to start a new world up or to give the built-in tutorial a try, but later any worlds you start and save will show up here.

There's a secret Nether Portal in the Minecraft sign in the tutorial!

You start with nothing in Minecraft

And there are things that want to kill you right off the bat

how to start a game

Ready to start a world?! Select "Create New World" from the "Play Game" menu, and take a gander at all the options you've got! Here's a big not-so-secret about Minecraft: there are just about an infinite number of possible worlds to try out, and not all are created equal. In fact, you'll find new environments that require different tactics in almost every world you start, which is one of the reasons Minecraft is such a popular game.

When preparing a world for play, you've got two sets of options to look at.

Make your selections

The Primary Options

These are the most important options for making your new world just how you want it, and they're the only ones you actually have to set. The first three, "Online Game," "Invite Only" and "Allow Friends of Friends" all have to do with playing single player or multiplayer. You can start a game by yourself no matter which of these are checked, but if you want other people to play with you, make sure "Online Game" is checked and then check the other two depending on who you want to be able to join.

"World Name" isn't too important, but it is what your world will be permanently saved as, so pick something memorable!

"Seed for the World Generator," however, is very important to how your world comes out. Seeds are numbers that the game uses to create your world, and they can either be set manually (if you want to play a seed you've heard about) or left blank for a random seed based on the time.

In Creative Mode you have access to every item and material in the game

You'll now need to set the type of game you're playing. For the Xbox 360 version, this means choosing between "Creative" or "Survival" modes and the two are exactly what they sound like. "Creative" mode is all about making things, and you get access to every single item and material in the game without having to find them. Additionally, you can fly and manipulate the world however you want. "Survival" mode, on the other hand, forces you to find and/or create items and structures from what's in the world around you, and all the while you'll be fighting against hostile monsters and the elements. This guide is mostly centered on "Survival" mode, though "Creative" mode is absolutely worth checking out too.

Finally, you need to set a difficulty level, for which you have four options:

Peaceful: No hostile mobs exist. You don't need to eat.

Easy: Hostile mobs are fewer and do less damage. Not eating does less damage.

Normal: The standard number of mobs spawn and do standard damage. Not eating depletes your health.

Hard: There are more monsters and they will seriously mess you up if they catch you, and not eating can kill you.

For your first game, we suggest trying either "Normal" or "Easy."

More Options

The "More Options" button lets you tweak your world a little more, though you can leave it alone if you want. Here you'll find eight more options to turn on or off, and these fall into the following categories:

Online Game Options: "Player vs Player" lets you decide whether multiplayer participants can hurt each other or not, while "Trust Players" is an option you can turn off if you don't want newcomers to be able to build or destroy until you say so. "Host Privileges" turns on the option for you, the host of the game, to have special abilities if you want them, but it also negates any achievements you get from playing.

Here's where you can tweak the game a bit more

Screenshot: Minecraft® ™ & © 2009–2013 Mojang/Notch.

You're just a few menus away from your first mine

The world that awaits you

Craft with a friend!

Fire and TnT: Turn these off if you want fire and TnT to do no damage.

World Options: If "Generate Structures" is turned off, you won't find any Villages, Nether Forts or Strongholds in your game, each of which is a structure you can find out more about in the "Navigating Villages and Structures" section of the guide. "Superflat World" makes everything flat, just like it sounds. "Bonus Chest" can make a big difference to how your first few days go. It spawns a chest near your starting point that contains quite a few usable items, meaning you don't have to make your own.

Using the above info, make your menu choices the way you'd like them to be, and then press "Create New World" to start up your very first world!

controlling your miner

Minecraft controls are pretty darn simple, and if you've ever played a First Person Shooter game, you're already familiar with the basic idea. For those that haven't, your RS (right stick) looks around the world, while the LS (left stick) moves you forward, backward and in any other direction in a straight line without changing which direction you're looking.

The lettered buttons on the right of your controller (X, Y, B and A) control Crafting, Inventory, Throw Item and Jump, respectively, while LB (left button) and RB (right button) cycle through items in your inventory tray at the bottom of your screen. Two of the most important buttons are LT (left trigger), which opens menus for Crafting Tables, Furnaces and other crafting mechanisms and eats food, and RT (right trigger), which uses the item in your hand to hit blocks and triggers mechanisms like buttons.

Check out the images below to see these and the few other controls as they're mapped out on your controller.

your first few minutes

You're here, what now?

Right, so you're in the world of Minecraft. You've got no items, no shelter and a whole wide world out there to explore. But what to do first? While you can really do whatever you want, if you want to survive your first day (and night!), you should do two things: look around, and gather resources.

This is a great starting location between two Biomes

A simple spawn point beacon

Looking Around

When starting a new game, the first thing to do is put a marker down where you started. To do this, dig out some dirt from the ground with your hand and stack it in a column. This will help a lot later. Now, simply look around a bit and see where you've started. Minecraft is split up into different environments called "Biomes," and each Biome contains specific plants, animals, resources and terrain-types. You can build and mine in any Biome, but some are much more convenient and safe when it comes to creating a shelter to live in. The number one priority is trees, because without trees, you aren't going to be able to craft important tools and items. After that, look for areas with water, animals and easily defendable terrain such as mountaintops. One good trick is to find a spot where two Biomes meet and build there. Remember though: nighttime comes fast, so don't spend too much time traveling on your first day.

Gathering Resources

On your first day out, you want to make every second count, so while you're looking for a nice place to set up a shelter, you'll need to be gathering resources. At the beginning of the game, certain resources are more important than others. The smartest order for gathering goes Wood>Cobblestone>Food>Wool, but if something is very close to you (say a Pig wanders by), take the opportunity to pick it up.

To gather Wood, you need to punch some trees. The noble art of tree-punching is what starts just about every game of Minecraft, and to do this, point the crosshairs at the wood of the trunk and punch the blocks until they break. This is the slowest way of collecting wood, however, and you'll want an Axe as soon as possible.

Two types of trees

When you've collected at least 3 Wood, open your crafting menu and create a set of four Wood Planks, then create a Crafting Table. The recipe for the Crafting Table is one block of Wood Planks in each of the four squares of the menu. You can then place your crafting table anywhere in the environment. Now, to make an Axe. Point at your Crafting Table after you place it and open the Crafting Table menu. You should then turn all of your remaining Wood into Wood Planks and turn at least 2 of your new Wood Planks into Sticks. Once you have at least 3 Wood Planks and 2 Sticks, you can create your first tool, an Axe!

Wooden Planks

Your first crafting table!

Your first shelter should be simple and effective

building a shelter

With your Axe, you can now chop down trees much quicker. Continue doing this until you have about 30-40 Wood (you may need to create another Axe if yours breaks), then break up your Crafting Table by chopping it, pick it up and move to where you want to build a house.

Place your Crafting Table and turn about 2/3 of your Wood into Wood Planks (you need about 60-100). Put the Wood Planks in your inventory tray, and start building a house! The quickest way to do this is to create a rectangular shelter at least 4 blocks long, 2 blocks wide and 4 blocks tall. Build the bottom layer first, then jump on top and run around it putting up the second layer. Repeat for the third and fourth layers, and then jump in.

A good first shelter

Doors are a necessity. You don't want those Creepers sneakin' in!

Wooden Pickaxe

A typical first mine. This one was a natural cave that was widened.

Before you fill in the hole with a ceiling, you need light, and light means Torches. Torches are created with one Stick and one Coal or Charcoal. To get Coal, you have to find a Coal deposit and mine it with a Pickaxe, and to get Charcoal, you need to burn Wood in a Furnace, which means you need to gather Cobblestone.

gathering more resources

At this point, you need to build your first Pickaxe, the most famous and useful tool in the game! To do this, open your Crafting Table menu up again and create the Wooden Pickaxe. (you may need to make more Wood Planks and Sticks to do this)

With your trusty new Wooden Pickaxe, you are now able to mine your first Stone (a big moment!). Leave your house by chopping a hole 2 blocks high and 1 block wide in the wall, and look around where you are. Try to find a hill or mountainside with exposed Stone. If you can't see any, you can just pick a spot and dig down until you hit some. Remember to leave a few blocks that you can jump on to get out.

At this point, you need at least 8 Cobblestone, but gathering around 20-30 won't hurt if you have time. Once you have some Cobblestone, head back to your shelter.

A shelter that's ready for night

It won't take long before your simple home starts to look like a mighty dwelling

Before you build a furnace, let's put a door on that home. Open your Crafting Table, and create the Wooden Door (this takes some Planks). Step outside your home again, select the door in your Inventory Tray and point your crosshairs at the hole in the side of your shelter. Use the Left Trigger to place the door, then open it and walk in.

Go to your Crafting Table again and move to the Chest icon. Push down on the D-Pad, and then create the Furnace when it shows up. Place the Furnace anywhere in your shelter, and then open it up with Left Trigger. Furnaces take fuel, which is something burnable like Wood or Coal. Put some of your remaining Wood in the top item slot, and then use Wood, Wood Planks or something else made of wood in the bottom one. You'll see the Furnace come on as it starts to turn your wood into Charcoal.

While this is happening, finish the roof to your home. Make sure it's fully enclosed, or else a Spider could fall on your head during the night!

Now, check your Furnace. Take the Charcoal from the Furnace, and open your Crafting Table back up. In the Tools section, you'll see Torches. Use all of your Charcoal up making Torches, and then start placing your Torches on the walls and ground around your home.

Once you've got a completed shelter, you can continue gathering resources until Nighttime. Soon enough, you'll start seeing the sun go down, which means Nighttime is about to arrive with all of its terrors. But no worries, because you've got a handy little shelter to protect you! Congrats on your first day in Minecraft.

nighttime

Here's the deal: when night falls on the world of Minecraft, things are going to try and kill you. A lot. All night long. This is because the monsters in Minecraft, known as "hostile mobs," can only survive when the level of light is low (except for Slimes, Spiders and the dreaded Creeper, which can survive in the day). Add that to the fact that hostile mobs spawn randomly at nighttime and then attack you on sight, and you've got yourself a bit of a dangerous situation for your character.

To put it simply, when that sun goes down, you had better be prepared to deal with the perils of night until that blissful moment when you see the light start to peek back over the horizon. If you're not prepared, you can be sure that your character is not going to survive.

This situation is very easy to fall into at night...

...As is this one

So, what can you do to protect yourself in the dark, dangerous Minecraft nighttime? Luckily, you've got quite a few options, and you should have no problem keeping safe and snug with even the most basic preparation during the day.

the necessaries

You need two things for certain if you're going to live to see another day in Minecraft: Shelter and Lighting.

Shelter

The Primary Number One Super Important Thing to have that will keep you safe from all of the Zombies, Skeletons, Endermen, Spiders and (shudder) Creepers at night is a nice shelter. You can read all the details on how to build a good basic shelter in the "Getting Started/Your First Day" section of this guide, but the basic idea is that you need an enclosed area with no open spaces to hide in. That's actually all you need to stay safe at night, but it'll be a dark, boring nighttime without at least a little light.

Lighting

Torches are your best friend in Minecraft, and you definitely need some in your shelter. Again, check out the "Getting Started/Your First Day" section to see exactly how to make a few torches. Another way torches are super useful at night besides letting you see (which is pretty darn useful, we'd say) is to keep monsters from spawning. Light in Minecraft is measured on a scale of 1-15, and monsters cannot spawn in any light level above 7. By placing torches in an area, you can keep monsters from spawning there, though they can still travel through it. To do this, you need to put torches so that there are no more than 11 blocks between them in a straight line and no more than 5 between them diagonally.

the secondary ideas

While you don't absolutely need these things, your nighttime experience will be a heck of a lot safer and more fun if you have them.

A Bed

This is the most useful tool to have at night, and it's one of the first things you should try and build in Minecraft. A Bed is a 2 block long item that can be placed in your world and slept in during the night, which instantly makes it day again. Not only that, but sleeping in a Bed sets your spawn point to that bed, meaning that when you die, you won't have to run back to your shelter!

To build a bed takes 3 Wood Planks and 3 Wool of any color. Wool is relatively easy to come by, as it drops when you kill Sheep. Use your Crafting Table to combine the Wood Planks and Wool, and set your Bed someplace where the sides are unobstructed. Then, just sleep in it when it's nighttime, and you'll skip right through the danger to daytime.

A nicely lit room

Everyone needs a bed!

Weapons & Armor

When you start a game in Minecraft, you're basically an unprotected weakling. Sad to say, but it's true. That doesn't have to remain the case though, as you can beef up your character's power through crafting weapons and armor to use in combat.

Basic weapons are easy to get early on, as you only need 1 Stick and 2 Wood Planks or Cobblestone to make a Sword. Do this as soon as you can, as it makes a huge difference in your attack and will often save your life during combat. In fact, even a Wooden Sword does four times the damage that punching does, and that damage rating goes up with better materials (except Gold).

Other weapons in Minecraft include Bows, Tools and Potions, each of which does differing amounts of damage, with Tools being the least effective. You can also use other items in the game, such as Cobwebs, Cactus, Snowballs, Fishing Rods and Buckets of Water or Lava to hinder or damage mobs in various ways, so get creative!

Armor, unlike weapons, can take a while to create because it requires a large amount of rare materials. Basic armor is made of Leather (dropped from a killed Cow), while better armor is crafted of Iron or Diamond (you can also use Gold, but this is not effective or recommended). Armor is worth making once you have enough Leather or a few extra Iron, as it makes an enormous difference in the amount of damage you can take.

With weapons and armor handy, you can actually brave the nighttime a little, though your chances at dying are still pretty high.

something to do

Once you've got a Bed, you don't need to deal with the night, but having to return to your Bed to sleep can get annoying after a while, especially if you're playing multiplayer (players must sleep at the same time). Because of that, it can be useful and fun to take the nighttime as a chance to do a few things.

A Crafter fully decked out in armor and weapons

On the attack!

The most obvious thing to do at night is to work on the inside of your shelter! Whether you decorate it, reorganize your materials, build more Crafting Tables, Furnaces or other useful items or even create another room or story, this is a great time to do this.

Nighttime is also a good time to refine your materials, such as making Iron Ingots out of Iron Ore or creating some extra Tools. Use your extra few minutes and get some stuff made!

Another great idea is to create a mineshaft that's accessible through your own home. You'll want to make sure this has a door on it to keep out mobs, but this can be an easy and efficient way to mine for resources while staying relatively safe.

Finally, once you're pretty confident in your weapons, armor and combat skills, you can go monster hunting at night…if you dare. Most mobs drop useful items when killed, and a small excursion out to hunt monsters can be very rewarding.

You need Torches, so you need Coal or Charcoal

Some mobs burn at night!

When you're ready, go mob hunting

A few walls and some Torches are all you need

nighttime facts

Here are a few facts about nighttime that can help you out:

Nighttime lasts 7 minutes of real time

Sunset/dusk is a short period of 1½ minutes real time during which players can go to sleep

Light decreases by 1 every 10 seconds during dusk

The natural light level at nighttime is 4

Crops can still grow at night

Sleeping through night, however, essentially stops time, so no crops grow and Furnaces pick up where they left off when you went to sleep

The day/night cycle continues even when you're in The Nether or The End

Spiders, Creepers and Slime are the only hostile mobs that do not die in the daylight

A random song will start to play at the beginning of each cycle of time

materials

Materials are everything in Minecraft, and we mean that quite literally. Except for player characters, NPCs (Non Player Characters, such as animals and mobs) and a few rare objects, everything you see in Minecraft is either a material or can be made with materials. This is what makes Minecraft so awesome: since everything breaks down into materials, you can destroy and build just about anything you want in the world.

This section of the guide will give you a quick look at the most important materials in the game, as well as a look at what you can make with them. Play enough Minecraft, and you'll come to know each and every one of these materials by heart. You'll know 'em, you'll learn to love 'em (or hate 'em—we're looking at you, Gravel) and soon enough you'll be squealing with glee every time you stumble on some precious, precious Diamond just like the rest of us.

building blocks

These are what the world of Minecraft is made up of, and they're what you'll mine and harvest to use in your own creations.

Dirt
Found: Overworld almost everywhere
Used In: Early shelters, farming
Best Tool to Use: Shovel
Look around you in the Overworld, and there's probably some dirt. Dirt is one of the most common blocks, but it's only real uses are for aesthetics and farming. You can make a shelter of it in a pinch, but it's always recommended to use something more stable (and better looking!) when you can. However, Dirt can have things grow on it, including "natural" materials like Snow, Mycelium and Grass as well as farmable materials like Trees and Wheat.

Wood

Types: Oak, Spruce, Birch
Found: Overworld in most Biomes except Desert, Plains and Mushroom
Used In: Wood Planks, which are needed for many items including tools and building materials
Best Tool to Use: Axe

Wood is without a doubt the most important resource in the game for one major reason: you need it to build tools. You also need it for many other items, but without tools, you're not going to be able to do much in Minecraft. You can find Wood just by looking around most worlds.

Stone

Types: Cobblestone, Stone
Found: Overworld, especially underground
Used In: Stone, Stone Bricks, other Stone building materials, Furnace, Stone tools, mechanisms
Best Tool to Use: Pickaxe

If you play Minecraft at all, you're going to end up with a whole lot of stone in the form of Cobblestone. Much of the Minecraft world, especially underground, is made of Stone or Cobblestone, both of which drop Cobblestone when mined. This stuff is required to craft a huge number of items, and you'll definitely want to keep a large stock of Stone tools on hand, as they're the easiest advanced tool to craft.

Gravel

Found: Overworld everywhere, usually between Stone and Dirt
Used In: Traps and nothing else. It is evil.
Best Tool to Use: Shovel
Drops: Flint

Gravel is evil. We say this because it's basically just there for variety and to make digging a bit more challenging. It's one of the only two blocks that drops when there's not a block below it (the other is Sand), and it can cause damage when falling far enough and can suffocate creatures it falls on that can't get out. Because of this, it's used in traps. It's only other useful feature is that it drops Flint, used in Flint and Steel.

Sand

Types: Sand, Sandstone
Found: Overworld near water and in Deserts
Used In: Glass, Sandstone, Sandstone Brick
Best Tool to Use: Pickaxe

Sand is the other block that, like Gravel, falls when there's nothing supporting it. Sand is the base block, from which Sandstone can be crafted, but you can also find naturally occurring Sandstone. Unlike Stone, Sandstone actually drops a Sandstone block when broken with a Pickaxe. Sand is mostly useful for making Sandstone to build with and Glass, which is also needed for Glass Panes.

Clay

Found: Overworld in water, usually in groups. Rare.
Used In: Clay Block, Bricks
Best Tool to Use: Shovel

Perhaps the rarest construction material block out there, Clay is found in water mixed up with Sand and Sandstone blocks, but is much less common than either of those. Clay is only used in two things: Clay Blocks and Bricks. Bricks can make a Bricks block, which is one of the more rarely seen building materials, as it takes a lot of Clay to get enough to make much.

Obsidian

Found: Overworld where running water has met standing lava, The End
Used In: Nether Portal, building shelter, Enchantment Table
Best Tool to Use: Diamond Pickaxe (nothing else works)

Obsidian is one tough material. In fact, you can only mine it with a Diamond Pickaxe, and its resistance level is 6000 (compare to Cobblestone's 30). That makes Obsidian hard to get, but it's necessary if trying to build a portal to the Nether or an Enchantment Table. You can find Obsidian only where running water has hit still lava, or you can create it by pouring water over lava. Because of its high resistance to damage, Obsidian makes for good safe rooms and walls.

Netherrack

Found: The Nether, all over
Used In: Nether Brick, can be lit on fire indefinitely
Best Tool to Use: hand, Pickaxe or Golden Pickaxe

This is what the Nether is made of, literally. It's incredibly quick to mine and is plentiful, which is nice if you like the way Nether Brick materials look. It has a very, very low damage resistance and can only be turned into Nether Brick, however, so it's not exactly the ideal for most players. Netherrack's ability to be lit on fire indefinitely makes it a common choice for traps and fireplaces.

Glowstone

Found: The Nether
Used In: Lighting
Drops: Glowstone Dust
Best Tool to Use: Any

A special block from the Nether, Glowstone is the best source of light in the game (level 15, Torches are 14). To get it, you'll have to break some Glowstone blocks and collect the Glowstone Dust that drops. This can then be converted back into Glowstone at a Crafting Table.

Soul Sand
Found: the Nether, often near large lava lakes
Used In: Traps and slowing mechanisms
Best Tool to Use: Shovel

Soul Sand is another unique Nether block that isn't used for much as of yet. Soul Sand's primary feature is that it slows down any creature that moves across it (items as well), making it useful in traps and mechanisms where slowing is desired. Its slowness effect is compounded when used in conjunction with water or ice.

End Stone
Found: The End
Used In: protection from the Ender Dragon
Best Tool to Use: Pickaxe

Another rarely seen block, End Stone is only found in The End, and its main use is as a building material when fighting the Ender Dragon. The Ender Dragon's attack can't destroy End Stone like it can other blocks, but End Stone is a lot easier to mine than Obsidian, making it the best choice for protective shelter in The End.

ores/minerals

When we're talking about the "mining" part of Minecraft, these are the things you'll be looking to find, for the most part. All ores and minerals form in "veins," or pockets that are usually surrounded by Stone, Dirt and Gravel (though sometimes water and lava too). They are much harder to find than most blocks, and they are used in most of the complex or advanced creations.

Note: You can craft solid blocks of each of the ores and minerals for use in decoration or certain recipes.

Coal
Types: Charcoal, Coal
Found: Charcoal—Burn Wood in a Furnace, Coal—the Overworld in formations at any level (1% of Stone blocks are Coal)
Used In: Torches, smelting, Fire Charge, running Powered Minecarts
Drops: 2/3 chance of experience dropping
Best Tool to Use: Pickaxe

The most plentiful ore is Coal, and that's good because you're going to need a whole lot of it. Coal is what makes Torches, which are the primary light source in your game. Without Coal, you won't have any torches, and you probably won't be able to see. Luckily, you can either burn Wood in Furnaces to make Charcoal or find Coal deposits easily in formations. Both work the same, despite their different names. Coal is also one of the best fuels for smelting in Furnaces (behind Lava Buckets and Blaze Rods). Covet your Coal, kids.

Iron

Found: Overworld from layer 1-63

Used In: Iron tools and armor, Buckets, Minecarts, Cauldron, Rails, Flint and Steel, Compass, Piston, Iron Door, and Iron Bars

Best Tool to Use: Stone Pickaxe or better required

If Diamond is the most coveted ore, Iron is the second, because Iron is necessary for so many important items. Whether building a railway with Minecarts, moving water or lava, setting a Nether Portal alight, trying to make a Map or even just mine Diamond and other rare materials, you'll need Iron. Iron is pretty common, luckily, though not nearly so as Coal. Look for it underground below sea level.

Gold

Found: Overworld from layer 1-32

Used In: Gold Ingot, which makes Gold tools and Armor, Golden Apples, Clocks and Powered Rails

Best Tool to Use: Iron Pickaxe or better required

Gold is a very rare ore, with only 0.1473% of the underground of the world having Gold Ore in it. It can be crafted into Gold Ingots, whose main use is to craft Clocks, Golden Apples and Powered Rails. Gold items like tools and armor are weak, but can be enchanted, though the benefits rarely outweigh the cost. Gold tools are however the fastest mining tools in the game, but they also break the easiest (even easier than Wood tools).

Diamond

Found: Overworld from layer 1-16

Used In: Diamond tools and armor, Jukebox, Enchantment Table

Best Tool to Use: Iron Pickaxe or better required

Diamond is king. No seriously, in Minecraft, you want Diamond, more Diamond and all the Diamond. This is because Diamond makes the second fastest and longest lasting tools in the game for mining and harvesting, it can mine any other block, it makes the best weapons and armor and it's necessary for some recipes. Unfortunately, Diamond is also by far the hardest material to find. Diamond is only in small deposits in the bottom 16 layers of the game, and it's only mineable with an Iron or Diamond Pickaxe. To find Diamond, you'll need to look in those low levels and try to find lava, which it's often nearby. A note: you need Diamond tools to mine Obsidian, which you need to get to the Nether, which you probably need to do to get to The End.

Redstone

Found: Overworld from layer 1-16

Used In: Redstone mechanisms and circuits, Compass, Clock, Note Block

Best Tool to Use: Iron Pickaxe or better required

Another mineral found deep, deep down, Redstone is much more common than Diamond, and in fact will drop multiple pieces of Redstone for each block. It's one of the most interesting materials in the game due to it being the thing you need to create powered circuits and mechanisms. Redstone placed by itself acts like a wire connecting mechanisms to each other and power (which comes from Redstone Torches, Buttons, Levers or Pressure Plates), and when used with those mechanisms and other Redstone items, you can create complex machinery and devices. Look for Redstone by lava.

Lapis Lazuli

Found: Overworld from layer 1-32

Used In: dying things blue

Best Tool to Use: Stone Pickaxe or better required

Lapis Lazuli is fairly rare in the game, but it also drops multiple pieces when it breaks, and it's not used for anything except to dye Wool blue. It's fun to come across, especially if you love blue, but it isn't as valuable as some of the other ores.

"natural" materials

These are materials you'll come across in the world that aren't used in building except indirectly. In fact, you can only even pick up water or lava, but all of these natural materials have particular features that are worth noting.

Water

Found: the Overworld in any area

Uses: farming, creating Obsidian, putting out fire, decoration, shelter defenses, damaging Endermen

Water is important in Minecraft. You need it to farm, first of all, but you also want to have some with you most of the time when exploring so that you can put yourself out if you light on fire. Water is also used in decorating, in building barriers or traps for hostile mobs and in creating Obsidian, which occurs when running water touches still lava. Endermen are also damaged by water easily, and it has a high blast resistance, making it a good tool for attacking and defending. Water can be carried in Buckets.

Lava

Found: Overworld, the Nether
Uses: Defenses, decorations, building trash cans, creating Obsidian

Lava is found in pools on the surface of the Overworld, in underground caves and, most commonly, all over the Nether. It damages almost all creatures that touch it, and it also lights them on fire. This makes it dangerous, but also useful as a defensive decoration. You need lava to make Obsidian, which happens when running water hits still lava. Its biggest use, however, is perhaps its ability to destroy unwanted blocks. You can then set up a pit of lava in your shelter to throw unwanted items into, where they will be destroyed.

Note: Bookshelves, Leaves, Wool, Fences (but not gates), Vines, TNT, tall grass, Wood Planks, and Wooden Stairs are flammable and will be lit on fire by lava.

Snow

Found: Cold Biomes in the Overworld
Drops: Snowballs

Snow is mostly a decoration that sits on top of blocks, but if broken, it drops Snowballs. These can be used to create Snow Blocks, which can then be used as decoration or to make Snow Golems.

Grass

Found: the Overworld
Drops: Grass Seeds

Similar to snow, grass doesn't do much, but it does break into Seeds. Seeds are used to grow Wheat, and are thus worth keeping in your stockpile.

Mycelium

Found: in the Mushroom Biome in the Overworld
Uses: Growing Mushrooms

Mycelium is another growing material that sits on top of blocks in the Mushroom Biome. It doesn't drop anything and can't be picked up, but it can be used to grow Mushrooms, which grow faster on mycelium.

craftable materials

Other than for building, materials are gathered in Minecraft in order to turn them into other items with your Crafting Table. Of these there are many, and since half of the fun is discovering what materials create what kind of items, we're just going to give a basic breakdown of the types of things you can craft in the game.

Weapons and Armor

Like tools, armor as well as one weapon (the sword) are made of different materials, each of which is better than the last. The order of strength goes Leather<Gold<Iron<Diamond. There is also Chain armor in the game, which is between Gold and Iron in strength, but there is no natural way to get this in Survival at the moment. The other weapon in the game is the Bow, which is a ranged weapon made from a Stick and String.

Tools

Of course, the most important thing to craft is tools. Without tools, you're going to have a very slow and incomplete experience, so they're very important to know about.

Tools in the game come in five varieties: Wooden, Stone, Iron, Gold and Diamond. Leaving out Gold tools, which break easily (though they mine quickest), the other tools are tough, mine quickly and can mine the most types of materials in this order Wooden<Stone<Iron<Diamond. In fact, you need a tool of the material before each in that order to even mine the next one.

Tools come in many varieties: Shovel, Hoe, Axe, Pickaxe, Shears and Fishing Pole. Some people consider Maps, Compasses, Buckets etc. to be tools, but we think it's simplest to stick with the definition that tools are items that are used to mine or harvest materials.

Material Refining

These are items that can be crafted to help craft other items. This includes:

Crafting Table: Your basic item-creation station

Furnace: Refines ores, makes Charcoal and cooks food

Enchantment Table: Enchants items with power-ups

Brewing Stand: Creates potions with buffs and debuffs as well as attacks

Cauldrons: Hold water, used to be for brewing before Brewing Stand was added

Mechanisms

Everything you use for Redstone devices! This includes Buttons, Levers, Pistons and more, and they're some of the more complex and difficult-to-master items in the game. Play around with a few and a bit of Redstone, and you can create anything from a food dispenser to a trapdoor to even a working computer.

Transportation

Rails, Minecarts and Boats fall in this category. This is everything you can create that helps you move without using your feet.

Decorations

Some folks are all about the building, some love adventure, and some love to design cool houses. Minecraft obliges this last group of Minecrafters by providing ample items to spruce up that shelter, including colored Wool blocks, Paintings and much more.

Food

Though not all food is crafted, some is, and others are cooked in the Furnace to make them better. Food is necessary in survival mode, and it comes in a wide variety of types. Food items are either used as ingredients in food that can be eaten, or they can be cooked or eaten themselves.

All Other Items

You'd think with a list this big that we'd be done, but nope! There are dozens of other items out there in the world of Minecraft, many of which are rare and difficult to acquire. We've covered everything we think is essential above, so we'll leave it to you to discover the other unique items in the game for yourself! Good luck, and here's a hint: keep on exploring. You never know what you'll find in the next chest.

inventions

If you've been playing Minecraft for a bit, there's a good chance that at some point you had to come up with a plan to overcome some problem or other in the game. Maybe you had to figure out how to pipe water to a new area, or you needed to build a staircase in a small space. If you've found yourself in that situation and came up with a working idea, congrats! You just joined the ranks of Minecraft inventors.

An intense Redstone invention

Elevators are possible!

what's a minecraft invention?

Only one of the most original and awesome parts of any game we've ever played! Inventions in Minecraft are pretty simple to define: they're things that people have built in the game in order to solve a problem or complete a task.

Most inventions fall into one of three categories: practical inventions, mob-based inventions or Redstone inventions. Practical inventions are all of those that do something that's maybe not too flashy to look at, but helps a lot in the game, such as infinite water in your home or a mechanism that makes Obsidian. Mob-based inventions are those that utilize mobs, usually farming them for drops or experience, but sometimes for other reasons like automated breeding. Redstone, of course, use Redstone, and they usually involve moving parts and lots of circuitry.

Here we'll show you how to make a few of the simple starter inventions. These are certainly not the only inventions out there, nor are they anywhere near the most complex. Instead, these are designed to get the ball rolling in your mind and give you some invention inspiration and skills. Try these out, and you might one day found that you just built an entire computer in game! Make us proud, Minecrafter.

A bordered water well

Another well in a home

The Infinite Water Well

No home is complete without one. The infinite water well is incredibly simple, but it's also one of the inventions that you're going to find yourself using time and time again. It puts a pool of water wherever you like it, and it will fill back up forever, no matter how many Buckets you take from it

All you need to build it is:
• 2 Buckets
• A space for a 2x2 hole

Make 2 Iron Buckets (takes 6 Iron Ingots) at your Crafting Table, and head out to find you some water. The easiest place is the ocean, because you'll need water you can pick up with the bucket (in other words, still water or water at the source of running water).

Pick up two Buckets worth of water, then go to where you want your infinite water well. You need to dig a 2x2 square that's 1 block deep, or you can build one with blocks. Take one Bucket of Water and pour it out into one corner of the hole, then pour the other Bucket of Water into the corner that's diagonally opposite. The flowing water will soon go still, and you'll have water forever!

Make sure you don't get too close to the trashcan!

The Trashcan

Pesky, pesky Gravel and Dirt, always filling up our inventories! Well those days are gone with the newfangled home Trashcan. The Trashcan uses the properties of certain materials to permanently destroy items, ridding them from your inventory in seconds.

Get:
- **1 Bucket of Lava or 1-4 Cactus blocks**
- **Any space in your home**

You can use any space for this because the size and shape of the Trashcan is up to you. We usually cut a block out where the wall meets the floor, then the block immediately below that one, and then two out from there. We then build Cobblestone walls on the sides of the trench we made, but that's just our preference. Basically, you just need a space that can hold the lava or Cactus, and preferably one you won't touch or fall into (and that the lava can't escape from!). Once you've got your space, just dump the lava in or place the Cactus. Note: Cactus can't have a block touching them except on the corners, so you'll have to keep the area clear. Once it's set up, try dumping a stack of blocks into your trashcan, and watch them disappear instantly.

The bottom of the mob grinder

The black block is where your mob spawner sits, and the blue block is where you put the hole to the area below

Basic Mob Grinder (Item Farm)

There are so many variations on inventions that kill mobs automatically that we literally could not count them all, and some of them get mind-bendingly complicated. All you're really looking to do, however, is create an area that forces mobs to be damaged and then collects their drops in a safe-to-access area. This is pretty easy to do, so here's one of the simplest mob grinders out there.

You need:
- **A mob spawner (found in Dungeons, Strongholds and randomly in the world, don't break it when you find it!)**
- **1 Bucket of Water**
- **An area at least 8x8x2 (8 wide, 8 long, 2 tall)**
- **An area 1 block below the first that's 3x3x4 (or 5x5x4 if you need to build a wall around the 3x3x4 space)**
- **2 Cactus blocks**

First build the top room around the mob spawner. You can't pick up mob spawners, so you'll have to build around the one you find. Hopefully, you'll find one that already has a room around it, but in case you don't, here's what to do.

The room itself can be any size, but you need at least an 8x8x2 area because this is how far a mob can spawn from a spawner. If there's a block outside of your grinder that's within that 8x8x2, a mob can spawn there. We recommend building a smaller room and surrounding the area with the mob spawner with these blocks. Smaller rooms are best for this, as the mobs are more likely to fall into your grinder, but you need to at least make sure that the area around the room is safe from mob spawning. Additionally, if you're using a Zombie or Skeleton spawner, this room should be dark.

The grinder prepares to grind

Items gathered for your convenience

Punch a 1-block hole in the floor of your mob spawner room (Note: if using a spawner for a wider mob, like a Spider, use a hole 2 blocks long) . Dig this hole down 4 more blocks, then widen the area 1 block around the hole so you have a 3x3x4 space. Make sure the only way between the mob spawner room and this room is the 1 block wide hole in the ceiling. On one side of the new room, punch a hole into the middle block 2 blocks from the ground. This is where your water will go. On the opposite side, knock out all 3 blocks on the bottom row. This is where your mob drops will be carried out of the grinder by the water.

You'll need to create a space for the drops to flow into on the outside of your 3x3x4 room, so it's a good idea to put the grinder near an area you've already excavated. Alternately, you can just build this entire mob grinder outside (though make sure the room with the spawner is dark if needed) and have the drops flow out onto the ground. We like to make a little wall around the water as it comes out of the grinder, making a pool full of items.

To make the grinder deadly, stack 2 Cactus blocks on top of each other in the center of your 3x3x4 room. This should be directly below the hole that leads to your spawner room with a 1 block gap between the top of the Cactus and the hole. Dump your Bucket of Water into the hole you punched into the back of your 3x3x4 room, and then get back to the mob spawner room you built above (repairing any holes you make in the grinder as you go). Leave the room, sealing any possible exits except for the hole to the Cactus.

You're done! As the mobs spawn and move around, they'll fall down the hole and be stuck on top of the Cactus. This will kill them, dropping the items into the water around the Cactus, which will carry it out of the slot you made on the opposite wall.

Remember: hostile mob spawners only turn on if you're within 16 blocks, so you'll need to be working around the area to turn on your new grinder.

You'll need to place a block behind the Dispenser in order to place one on top of it

The completed fridge

The Fridge

An absolutely simple and really fun little build, the fridge is a nice way to make food retrieval easy and aesthetically pleasing. You can set this up in under a minute, if you have the right items

You need:
- **1 Button**
- **Food of any kind**
- **1 Dispenser**
- **2 blocks of any kind that can take a Button (almost all can)**
- **1 block of any kind**

Pick a spot in your home that you frequent and that has space for a 1 block hole in the ground and 2 blocks above (so 1x1x3). Dig a hole there 1 block deep and put your Dispenser so that it faces the way you'd like the food to come out. Then, place 1 block of any type exactly 1 block behind and one block above the Dispenser on the opposite side that it's facing. Now take your 2 blocks that you want to have your button and place one against the first block you placed so that it goes on top of your Dispenser. Place the second block above this one, and break the first block that you placed 1 block behind and 1 block above the Dispenser. You should now have a stack of two blocks on top of your dispenser. Put a button on the bottom block, and then push it. Food will fly right out at you!

Bye, you creepy Creeper!

Step 1

The Trapdoor

Ready for a bigger build? This is one of the easiest Redstone builds, but it's still a bit of a doozy for those who aren't familiar with the material. Try this one out as a good way to learn the basics of Redstone. For this tutorial, we're going to show you the way this works in a space without any other construction around it. Once you've correctly built it, you should be able to figure out how to implement it in your shelter or other builds.

Get:
• 1 Sticky Piston
• 2 blocks of anything except Gravel or Sand
• 7-15 Redstone (at least)
• 1 Lever
• 3 Slabs of any kinds (at least)

Dig a hole 4 blocks long and one block deep (4x1x1). Place your Sticky Piston so there are 2 blocks between it and one end of the hole. Have the Piston so the green side is facing the end with 2 empty blocks. Now place 1 of your blocks on the end of the Sticky Piston (on the side with the green stuff on it). On the empty block on the other side of the Piston, put down one square of Redstone. On the block immediately 1 block behind and above the Redstone (outside of your trench), place a Lever. Pull the lever, and the Piston should extend with the block. If it doesn't, your Redstone connection is broken somehow, so you'll need to redo the previous steps.

Step 2

Step 3, your trap is on!

This method can be applied to your home's front door with some doing

Next, go place slabs over the block with the Redstone, the Piston itself and its extended arm. Go back and pull the Lever again, and then jump in the hole at the end of the trench left when the Piston retracts. If you want this trapdoor to kill players or mobs, dig this hole down pretty far, or place a Cactus or lava in it. If you just want the trapdoor to lead to another room, you'll want to build your room beneath it.

When building this for your house, you'll probably want to figure out a way to get the Lever inside your home. You can make the Redstone trail from the Lever to the Piston for up to 16 blocks, so get creative with how to put your Lever inside! It'll probably require some tunnel digging and trial-and-error, but it can definitely be done.

Farm well!

Mine better!

mining & farming

Here they are, mining and farming. The meat and the potatoes of Minecraft. If you don't mine and at least kill a Cow or rip up a Wheat or two, you are not Minecrafting. In fact, you're probably just standing still, dying slowly of hunger. We don't want you to die slowly of hunger, young Minecrafter. We want you to live, and mine, and farm…and probably get killed by a Creeper, but then mine and farm again!

Like most things in Minecraft, you can just take a Pickaxe to a random chunk of ground or a Sword out looking for food mobs and hope for the best, and sometimes that's a lot of fun. But, if you want to get the most out of your mining and farming efforts, then you should know a few things.

All you need to mine is a good bit of stone

And soon you'll have something like this

mining

Mining is broken down into two types: clearing an area, and ore mining.

Clearing an Area Mining

Just like it sounds, this is when you're not necessarily looking for ore; you're mainly trying to clear a space for a shelter or some other reason. This is fairly straightforward, but there are some ideas that can help you do this quickly and more efficiently

- As always, don't dig straight up or straight down. This is the time when players are most likely to do this, so it's worth repeating.

- Cut out the shape of the thing you're making first. Designing a good area works best when you make sure of the dimensions before you start the heavy digging. Just mine out the outline of what you want to build and the rest will go much quicker.

- You can mine 4 blocks forward and 3 down from the one you're standing on without moving. Mining as much as you can in a straight line makes for more efficient mining.

- Stay aware. You never know when you might crack into a cave, Stronghold or lava pit. Be ready.

- Take the ore you see. Don't let the plan keep you from grabbing some ore. Get ore as soon as you see it, then replace the blocks if you need to keep a certain shape going.

- Create stopgaps with Doors. Don't just mine open tunnels all the time. Put Doors in and even create little mini-bases, and you'll mine much safer and faster.

Some gold in a cave

A proud miner stands by his Diamonds

Ore Mining

This is the big one, guys. Ore is essential to Minecraft. Ore is what you want, what you need and what you will get if you try hard and have a little luck.

The Basic Idea: You're looking for ore deposits, and all ore is created right when you start your world. It's placed around your world according to certain rules and algorithms, and there are places it won't spawn, places it might spawn and places it's likely to spawn. Each ore is different. You need to know where each ore spawns and then look for it in those places.

Where Ores Spawn: Here's your guide to where types of ore spawn.

Ore	Layers Found (overall)	Most Commonly Found on Layers
Coal	Any level with Dirt or Stone	Any, but lower layers can contain more
Iron	2-67	5-54
Gold	2-33	5-29
Lapis Lazuli	2-33	14-16
Redstone	2-15	5-12
Diamond	2-15	5-12

Basic Techniques: Beyond just rushing into a big, beautiful pile of stone and hacking away at it with a Pickaxe, you should prepare yourself and have at least some idea of a plan before you go charging in. Try these techniques.

Prepare your inventory. Make sure you have most of your inventory clear, but you need to bring a few things for even basic mining.

We recommend a mining kit of the following:
1. No less than 3 Stone Pickaxes for basic work

2. 1 Iron Pickaxe

3. At least 64 Torches

4. Food, preferably Steak, Porkchops or Cake (for their hunger saturation boost)

5. Some Wood (for Torches, an emergency Crafting Table, new tools etc.)

6. Some Coal

7. A Sword and armor if possible

You will find mobs in your mines. Be ready.

This mineshaft cracked right into the End Portal room of a Stronghold

Bringing much more is not recommended, as you'll need your inventory full for things you pick up/mine.

- Plan out the location and length of your excursion. If you're looking for a certain ore, you know that you'll need to go to the level it spawns in. If you're mining close to home, keep in mind where your existing structures are so that you don't accidentally run a mineshaft into one. If you're going out to a new cave or area, make sure you know or mark the way back.

- Keep it tidy. It might seem like a hassle while you're doing it, but trust us; when you go back to an area you've already mined, and you didn't keep the excavation tidy and easily understood, you'll wish you had. You'll get a lot more out of mining if you clean up and light your tunnels as you go instead of leaving them dark and confusing. Make signs if you have to!

- Watch out for mobs. They spawn in the dark, and they will get you if you're not paying attention.

- If you break into or come across a big, new area, mark the entrance to your existing mine as much as possible. Light that thing up with torches, because it is very easy to forget the way back.

A completed staircase to the Bedrock

Staircase in progress

Advanced Techniques

Once you've got the hang of basic mining, try some of these tried-and-true methods for ultra-efficient ore discovery.

The Staircase Method: Most veteran Minecrafters will tell you that this is one of the best and most common methods for quick ore discovery, and it's easy to do. All you do is create a staircase from where you start mining all the way to the bedrock. Some players prefer a straight diagonal staircase, while others go for a spiral; either is fine. You may crack into a tunnel, cave or even a Stronghold on the way. If you can, mark this and keep digging your staircase until it's finished. If you can't (say, you crack into the top of a ravine), start a new staircase instead of trying to move this one over. The reason for all of this is that it greatly simplifies mining at deeper levels. If you have a staircase that accesses every level, you can head directly to the level you need depending on the ore you're looking for. Plus, it's very easy to see where you've already explored and to start in on a new area by building staircases this way.

The results of branch mining: Diamonds!

The branch mining hallway grows

A branch

Branch Mining: Combined with the Staircase Method, branch mining is the simplest way to hugely increase your chances at finding good ore. It's also fairly easy, yay! To branch mine, pick a level at which the ores you want can be found. Typically this is layer 15 and below. When there, mine out a hallway 2 blocks wide and 3 blocks tall. Make this as long as you want, just make sure it goes straight. When you've got a decently long hall, go back to the front. Now, aim at one of the first blocks on the wall of the hall and mine a new hall (the branch hall) perpendicular to the original hall. This new branch hall should be only 1 block wide and 3 blocks tall. Mine it back about 7-12 blocks, then put a torch at the end. Go back along the new hall and mine out any ores you find, then go back to the main hall. Looking at your new 1 block wide branch hall, move to the right 2 blocks, and make another 1 block wide branch hall off of the main hall, going back the same amount of blocks and taking any ore you find. Repeat this process on both sides of the main hall until you reach the end, then either extend the main hall and repeat or start a new one somewhere else. What this does is to reveal the most blocks with the least digging, meaning you're more likely to see ore with less work and time put in.

The Tutorial world has a great example of an animal farm

Sheep: they love Wheat

farming

Farming also has two distinctive types, but the two types of farming are quite different from each other. One revolves around the capture of animals to breed and harvest meat and drops from, and the other revolves around planting and harvesting crops of plants.

Animal Farming

Don't worry, this isn't about to get all Orwellian. Animal farming is pretty simple in Minecraft, though some automated breeder inventions can take things to a whole 'nother level. What you need to do for an animal farm is fourfold: find the animals and get them to follow you, put them in an enclosure, breed them and then harvest them.

1. Find and Follow: Most peaceful animal mobs in Minecraft have a certain item that they really like, and when you hold it, they'll follow you. This is ultra-convenient for animal farming, as otherwise you have to shove animals one by one into your pens, or just hope they walk in on their own. Here's what animal follows what item:

- **Wheat: Cows, Pigs, Sheep and Mooshrooms**
- **Wheat Seeds: Chickens**
- **Bone (use on to tame): Wolves**

You can tell that animals are ready to breed when they display the floating hearts

A baby cow!

2. Put 'em in a Pen: Now that you've got some animals following, you need a place to put them. If you haven't built one already, just stick them in your home and close the door for now. Building pens is what Fences were made for, and this is where you should use 'em. Mobs need to be pretty close to each other to ensure breeding, so make a pen for each type of mob, and make them pretty small (maybe 8x8 at the largest, but more often smaller). Use Gates on each pen in order to get in and out, and remember that some mobs are hard to get in through a 1 block wide hole, so make double Gates if necessary. It's also a good idea to put all the pens near each other, and then fence around the entire section of pens. This makes it less likely that any mobs will get out, and it gives you a space to let some roam a bit if you need to do so.

3. Breed those Guys: Breeding is a necessity for any good farm because it allows you to turn your animals into renewable resources. There's not a lot of point in going out and collecting animals just to kill them, and then have to do it again, right? To breed animals, you simply need to find the right item to feed them, then feed two of them in the same area. They'll find each other, breed, and a new little baby animal will spawn!

Here's what each animal needs to breed:
- **Wheat: Cows, Pigs, Sheep, Mooshrooms**
- **Any seed (not just Wheat Seeds): Chicken**
- **Any meat: Tamed Wolves**

4. Time for the Harvest: Yes, they may be cute when they're bouncing around in your pens, but you need that food! To harvest meat and items from animals, simply kill them. You can light them on fire to kill them and have their meat drop already cooked (if they drop meat), but this method doesn't drop experience. Use a Sword, and take a few out. The key here is to make sure you leave at least two animals of each species alive so that they can keep breeding later. A note: there's no reason to kill Tamed Wolves. They don't drop any items, and besides, they're your friends!

A cool-lookin' farm on the side of a castle

Tree farming with friends

Plant Farming

The primary plants for farming in Minecraft are Wheat, trees, and Pumpkins and Melons. You can also farm Sugar Cane, Mushrooms, Nether Wart and Cactus, but these are the plants that you're most likely to need and to farm in your game.

Wheat Farms: Wheat is probably the most commonly farmed plant (it's between Wheat and trees), and it's simple to farm. Wheat requires a light level of 9 or above and what's called farmland, which is what a block of Dirt turns into when you use a Hoe on it. For best Wheat growth, it should be no more than 4 blocks from a source of water as well. Wheat takes a variable amount of time to grow, but grows fastest under conditions where it's well-lit and on hydrated farmland. Harvested Wheat drops 0-3 Wheat Seeds when cut, making it a renewable resource. Use Torches or Glowstone near Wheat in order to make it grow even without sunlight.

Tree Farms: Wood is a hugely important resource in Minecraft, so tree farms can make your virtual life a lot easier. Like Wheat, trees need light, but they don't need water to grow, so again use Torches to grow trees. The easiest tree to grow is the Oak, and the easiest way to grow it is to make a 5x5x2 space of Dirt. In each corner, dig a hole 1 block down and plant an Oak Sapling in each hole. Put 3 Torches to a side, and the trees will grow easily. Trees usually drop Saplings, making it easy to replace them.

Wheat, Melons and Pumpkins need water and farmland

Set up your farm in this pattern

Melon/Pumpkin Farming: Pumpkins and Melons are both farmed in the same way. Pumpkins and Melons work best on farmland with hydration, like Wheat, but they grow differently. When planted, their seeds make a stem, which when mature grows a Melon or Pumpkin in one of the 4 adjacent blocks. This means you need to leave at least one space and preferably more around a planted Pumpkin or Melon Seed. These also produce Seeds when harvested.

You can build an advanced farm by building it in tiers. By building the same shape of farm one on top of the next (leaving a little space between for movement and lighting it up with torches, of course). You only need one source of water if you let it flow down from one to the next!

navigating villages & structures

The village Blacksmith

Villages often have farms

If there's one thing that Minecraft is all about besides building, it's exploring, and this game does not slouch when it comes to giving you cool things to find. In fact, even a player that's plugged hundreds of hours into Minecraft can climb just one more mountain or break into just one more cavern and come across a gorgeous view that they've never seen in the game.

The world you see in Minecraft is essentially broken down into natural environments (Biomes) and environments spawned from building materials (Structures). In the Xbox 360 version of Minecraft, there are currently four major Structures and two minor Structures, each of which has its own rules for where it can occur, what type of creatures populate it and what can be found or done within it. Knowing this info can make a big difference in your gameplay, especially when attempting to survive at the beginning of a game or when looking for certain items later on. There's nothing like coming across a Chest of Diamond right when you need it!

Note: when exploring just about any of these, except the Village, you'll want to bring plenty of Torches or other items to mark your path, or you most definitely will get lost.

Village by night

Villages are great places to find resources

Item	Quantity	Weight	Chance
Bread	1 – 3	15	62%
Apple	1 – 3	15	62%
Iron Ingot	1 – 5	10	47%
Iron Sword	1	5	27%
Iron Pickaxe	1	5	27%
Iron Helmet	1	5	27%
Iron Chestplate	1	5	27%
Iron Leggings	1	5	27%
Iron Boots	1	5	27%
Oak Sapling	3 – 7	5	27%
Obsidian	3 – 11	5	27%
Gold Ingot	1 – 3	5	27%
Diamond	1 – 3	3	17%

villages

If you're running around the Overworld (the part of the game that you spawn in), and you see a cluster of houses and think "Hey, I didn't build that!", you probably just found a Village. Villages are collections of buildings populated by Neutral Villagers.

Where

Villages only spawn in Plains or Desert Biomes. They tend to spawn where it's flat, but they can also spawn on hills and across ravines, which can make for strange set-ups.

Structures

Depending on the available space, the game will place certain structures in a Village. The Hut, Butcher's Shop, Small House and Large House are simple structures made of Wood, Wood Planks and Cobble, and they usually contain a Villager or two. The Watch Tower and Church are taller structures with great views and a Villager, and you can also find Wells and Lamp Posts (made of one Black Wool block and some Torches). The most important Village structures, however, are the Farms, Library and Blacksmith, which contain useful items.

Mobs

In the Xbox version, the only mobs native to Villages are the basic Villager, and as of right now, they don't do much except wander around. They won't attack, and they don't build.

Materials

Villages are excellent places to raid for building materials in a pinch, as they're made of things like Wood Planks and Cobblestone. The best resources, however, are found at the Farms, the Library and the Blacksmith. Farms yield Wheat and Wheat Seeds, which means you can easily make Bread or start your own Wheat Farm. Libraries contain Books (helpful for Enchanting) and a Crafting Table you can snatch up. The Blacksmith, however, has a couple Furnaces and the true treasure: a Chest of items. Check out the graph to the left to see what goodies you can expect in a Blacksmith's Chest.

A Stronghold library

Beware of mobs in Strongholds

strongholds

At some point in the game, you'll either accidentally pop into one of these (often massive) structures, or you'll need to find one to get to The End. Strongholds can sometimes be small, but usually they're huge, confusing and highly dangerous. There are only three Strongholds per world.

Where

Find a Stronghold by throwing an Eye of Ender. The direction it flies toward is the direction of a Stronghold. If you don't have an Eye of Ender, you're going to have to just dig around until you crack into one. Strongholds are always at least 640 blocks from your start point and no farther than 1152, and they also often intersect sections like Ravines, Mineshafts and Caves.

Structures

Strongholds are mostly mazes of hallways, stairs and rooms, but they also include a few specific structures of note. These include Store Rooms, Libraries and the End Portal Room. Store Rooms are exactly what they sound like: an area that contains a Chest of useful stuff. Libraries are rooms full of Bookshelves and Cobwebs, and they come in one-story and two-story sizes. They also contain chests at the end of one or two bookshelves, depending on the size of the Library. The End Portal room is the only place in the world the player can get to The End, which is done by placing Eyes of Ender into the blocks of the End Portal, a structure that sits above a pool of lava and is guarded by a Silverfish Monster Spawner.

Mobs

Fair warning: Strongholds are dangerous. They can contain just about every hostile mob in the Overworld, including Zombies, Skeletons, Spiders, Creepers and Silverfish. Silverfish are especially dangerous, as they can live in blocks called Monster Eggs that are disguised as normal blocks, and they attack in groups when one is damaged near others.

Materials

Large parts of Strongholds are built out of materials that are hard to come by elsewhere, such as Iron Bars, Iron Doors, Buttons, and special Stone blocks like Mossy or Cracked Stone. Even better, the Chests in Strongholds carry some great items, with possibilities including Ender Pearls, Apples, Bread, Coal, Redstone, Armor, Iron Ingots, Iron Swords, Iron Pickaxes and, rarely, Diamond, Golden Apples or Saddles.

If you find an Abandoned Mineshaft, be ready for Cave Spiders

Lucky players may find an Abandoned Mineshaft early and strip it of its Wood and other resources

abandoned mineshaft

These are just what they sound like: mineshafts that spawn as if someone else had built them and then abandoned them.

Item	Quantity per stack	Chance
Bread	1 - 3	20% (1/5)
Pumpkin Seeds	2 - 4	13% (2/15)
Melon Seeds	2 - 4	13% (2/15)
Iron Ingot	1 - 5	13% (2/15)
Coal	3 - 8	13% (2/15)
Redstone	4 - 9	7% (1/15)
Gold Ingot	1 - 3	7% (1/15)
Lapis Lazuli	4 - 9	7% (1/15)
Diamond	1 - 2	4% (1/25)
Rails	4 - 8	1.3% (1/75)
Iron Pickaxe	1	1.3% (1/75)
Enchanted Book	1	??% (??/??)

Where
Randomly placed underground, especially intersecting with ravines and caves.

Structures
Mineshafts are simply hallways, stairways, crossings and rooms, often with Rail Tracks, supports and Minecarts in them.

Mobs
All mobs that can spawn in darkness have a chance of being in a Mineshaft, with the added danger of the smaller Cave Spider, which spawns from Monster Spawners and is unique to Abandoned Mineshafts. These little guys are poisonous, so watch out!

Materials
If you plan on making anything out of Rails, breaking them up in Mineshafts is the most efficient method. Other simple materials such as Wood Planks, Fences and Torches can be found, as well as Chests, usually in Minecarts. See the chart at the left for likely Chest items.

Two-chest Dungeons are rarer than one-chest Dungeons

Get ready to fight if you find a Dungeon

Item stack	Chance of of spawning	Chance of finding a stack	Number in stack
Saddle	1/12	46.6%	1
Iron Ingot	1/12	46.6%	1-4
Bread	1/12	46.6%	1
Wheat	1/12	46.6%	1-4
Gunpowder	1/12	46.6%	1-4
String	1/12	46.6%	1-4
Bucket	1/12	46.6%	1
Enchanted Book	1/120	46.6%	1
Redstone	1/12	26.4%	1-4
13 disc	1/12	5.8%	1
cat disc	1/12	5.8%	1
Golden Apple (Normal)	1/120	0.6%	1

dungeon

Small rooms randomly placed about the map, Dungeons contain a Monster Spawner and a Chest or two of items.

Where

Just about anywhere, but often in caves. Look for Mossy Stone and Cobblestone: those two together usually indicate a Dungeon.

Structures

Nothing more than one simple room!

Mobs

There will probably be tons of mobs of whatever type of Monster Spawner is in there (Zombie, Skeleton or Spider). Beware!

Materials

Just Cobble and Mossy Stone and the Monster Spawner, besides what's in the Chest.

Nether Fortresses are not to be lightly trifled with

A Zombie Pigman stands guard over a crop of Nether Wart

nether fortresses

The only Structure found in the Nether, these are enormous, hugely dangerous and are the only place to find Nether Wart and Blazes. They're not too hard to find, but getting out alive requires great gear, patience and skill.

Where
The Nether, of course! Walk around long enough, and you're likely to find one, especially in big rooms, and when you do, the other Nether Forts will be laid out to the north and south in strips.

Structures
Nether Fortresses are comprised of tower-like structures connected by bridges. There are a few special rooms in the Forts: a stairwell with Nether Wart in it (the only place to find it), rooms with Blaze Spawners (also unique) and halls or rooms with Chests.

Mobs
You're most likely to come across Skeletons, Blazes and Magma Cubes in Nether Fortresses, while Ghasts may float above the bridges and Zombie Pigmen might be nearby. The rule for Nether Forts is to go in heavily armored and with the best weapons possible, as you will be attacked.

Materials
Besides the Nether Brick they're made of, which is immune to Ghast fireballs, and the items that spawn in chests (Iron Ingots, Gold Ingots, Golden Chestplates and Swords, Saddles, Flint and Steel, Nether Wart and Diamonds are possible), Nether Forts are also the only place to get Blaze Rods (from killing Blazes) and Nether Wart, both of which are essential for crafting certain items (especially potions). You can also get Glowstone Dust from Blazes, occasionally.

friends & foes

It only takes a few seconds in Survival Mode to realize that your character in Minecraft is not alone. Nope, the world of Minecraft is a full one, teeming with everything from tiny Chickens to Wolves to Zombie Pigmen to the giant Ghast, and if you're going to thrive in this crowded land, you're gonna need to know a bit about these creatures, known as "mobs."

Notes:

1. **This section focuses on location, behavior, drops and combat. For breeding, see the Mining & Farming section.**

2. **The Attack stats are approximate. Attack can change somewhat depending on circumstances and exact numbers have yet to be confirmed for the Xbox 360 version of the game.**

3. **Health, Armor and Attack are measured in half-icons, so 1 "heart" icon = 2 Health, one "sword" icon = 2 Attack, and one "chestplate" icon = 2 Armor.**

peaceful mobs

There are quite a few mobs out there that won't ever attack you, no matter how many times you punch them in the face or otherwise pester them. These mobs are considered "peaceful."

Sheep

Sheep are everywhere, they are not smart and you will need them for Beds. Sheep tend to spawn in flocks and then roam about, and since they can both jump 1 block high and swim, they end up all over the place.

Sheep are usually white (81.836% chance) but can also spawn as dark grey, light grey, or black (5%), brown (3%) or pink (0.164%), and whatever color they are is the color of Wool you will get from them. Wool can be gathered either by killing the Sheep or by using Shears on it (1 block for killing, 1-3 for shearing). You can also dye sheep to change the color of their Wool.

Chicken

Chickens may be small and easy to kill, but they also drop a ton of useful items and are easy to farm. You usually find Chickens spread out across the ground and water, and they can fall without taking damage, so they can end up in deep pits and ravines.

Chickens drop three potential food items: Eggs (used in cooking), Raw Chicken (2 units of the food bar, 1.2 hunger saturation [see Farming & Mining for more info], 30% chance of food poisoning) or Cooked Chicken (3 food units, 7.2 hunger saturation) if it was killed by fire. Chickens also drop Feathers, which are used in crafting Arrows.

Cow

Another pack wanderer, Cows often spawn in groups of 4-10 then wander off, sometimes even falling down cliffs and killing themselves.

Cows are one of the best sources of food, as Raw Beef gives 3 food units and 1.8 hunger saturation (no risk of poison), Steak gives 4 food units and 12.8 hunger saturation and Milk is used to cure status effects like poison and in cooking Cakes. Steak is the most balanced food item in the game, and Milk is infinite, making Cows very good to farm. Their other drop, Leather, is used in crafting the lowest level of armor.

Mooshroom

A rarer version of the Cow, the Mooshroom is a Cow that's been infected by Mushrooms. You can only find these guys in the uncommon Mushroom Biome, but they're even better than Cows for food and materials.

This is because, in addition to what a Cow drops, you can also get infinite Mushroom Stew (3 food units, 7.2 hunger saturation). On top of that, if you ever really need Mushrooms, you can use Shears on the Mooshroom and get 5.

Pig

Pigs spawn just about everywhere that's not underground, and their initial group is 3-4 pigs, so you can often find quite a few together.

Pig meat comes as Raw or Cooked Porkchops, and it gives identical health benefits to Raw Beef and Steak, respectively (3 food units, 1.8 hunger saturation / 4 food units, 12.8 hunger saturation), making Pigs a good source of food.

It is possible to find a Saddle in a Chest, put it on the Pig and ride it around. At this time, there's no way to control the Pig when riding, but that should come in a later update. Also, on the very rare occasion that lightning strikes within 3-4 blocks of a Pig, it will turn into a Zombie Pigman.

Wolf

Though they start out neutral and will become hostile if attacked (and will attack in groups), Wolves can be "tamed" by feeding them Bones. You'll know a Wolf is successfully tamed when it gets a collar around its neck and starts following you.

Tamed wolves follow the player and attack any mobs that attack the player or are attacked by the player except Creepers. They are most effective versus Zombies and Skeletons, less against Spiders, Cave Spiders and Endermen and almost not at all against Creepers, Magma Cubes and Slimes.

You can tell the health of a Wolf by the angle that its tail is pointing. A tail that is all the way up means full health, and all the way down means very low health, with corresponding positions in-between. To raise the health of your Wolf, feed it any meat, including Rotten Flesh (which won't hurt it).

Wolves also have special behavioral traits when it comes to mobility. A Wolf told to follow you that gets outside of a 20x20x10 block from the player will automatically teleport to the player, unless there's no room for it to do so. Additionally, you can tell a wolf to "sit" with Left Trigger, which makes it stay where it is until otherwise ordered.

Squid

The only water mob out there, the Squid will not attack and just drops Ink Sacs. They do make cool pets if you can trap them, though.

Villager

Villagers hang out in, not surprisingly, Villages, and as of Minecraft Xbox 360 update TU11, they don't trade, build or have any other interaction with the player except that you can hurt and kill them. Future updates may change this.

Zombie Pigman

All over the Nether, you'll find Zombie Pigmen, usually in groups. They spawn in fours, but can gather together in larger groups, and they hang out in most parts of the Nether.

Like Villagers, this mob is humanoid and initially neutral to the player, but unlike Villagers, Zombie Pigmen most definitely will attack you if you hurt one. In fact, attacking a Pigman alerts any other Pigmen within a 32 block radius, who will all go hostile and come at the player with Swords.

hostile mobs

Now, these are the guys in Minecraft who want nothing more than to bite you, poison you, shoot you full of arrows, light you on fire, punch you in the face, blow you up and otherwise attempt to make you no more. Even with the best gear, a few of these guys ganging up on you can mean a quick death, often far from home, especially if you don't know their tendencies and weaknesses. Get familiar with these guys as much as possible, and it most definitely will save your life.

Creeper

Ah, the Creeper. He's the unofficial mascot of the game, the sneakiest mob and the one you'll find yourself most dreading.

When Creepers get within two blocks of you (so one separating), their "countdown" starts, and you have 1.5 seconds before it blows up all of the blocks in about a 6x6x6 area around it. Yep, it's a pain. The only warning you get for this is a slight "hiss" sound when it gets close, and since they will attack any players they see within 16 blocks and are good at finding paths to you, it's pretty likely that you'll have at least one Creeper death in your Minecraft experience. This is made even more likely by the fact that they can survive in daylight, unlike most hostile mobs.

The good news is that Creepers can't blow up when they see you through Glass or a Door, and if you kill them from a distance or before they can do their countdown, they will die without exploding and will even drop Gunpowder, which you can use to make TNT. A harder drop to get from a Creeper is a Music Disc, which requires the Creeper be killed by a Skeleton's Arrow.

Because of their ability to blow up your hard work, it's best to protect yourself from Creepers by paying attention to your surroundings and building safely where they can't get to you. Because, as they say, that'ssssss a very nice house you've got there... It'd be a sssssshame if anything were to happen to it.

Spider

You're gonna see a lot of Spiders. Spiders are neutral until they've been exposed to darkness or attacked. This means that a Spider found in daylight will be neutral, but if he happens to wander into a dark area, he's gonna go hostile and stay that way. Spiders that start off in dark areas and move to light will remain hostile, however.

Despite their small attack, Spiders are dangerous because they can climb walls as if all blocks had Ladders on them and they can jump up to 3 blocks high. They also can see players through walls, meaning that if there's a hostile Spider within 16 blocks of you, it knows you're there and is trying to get to you, and they can even fit through one block high spaces.

To be safe around Spiders, wear armor, carry weapons and make sure your shelter is enclosed and well-lit. If you do kill a Spider, it may drop the very useful String or Spider Eyes.

Spider Jockey

A very rare mob, these have a 1% chance of spawning anytime a Spider does. They include a Skeleton archer riding on top of a Spider, both of which otherwise behave normally and take damage individually. Because of this, Spider Jockeys spawn, move and see like Spiders, though the Skeleton will simply attack anytime it sees you, whether the Spider is hostile or not. On top of that, the Skeleton can suffocate or burn in daylight, leaving the Spider on its own.

Skeleton

Skeletons are major pests in Minecraft because they spawn just about everywhere there's darkness and they attack with arrows from a distance. If you're being attacked in a dark cave and you can't see where it's coming from, then you've probably found a Skeleton.

Skeleton attacks don't do huge damage, however, and can even be entirely prevented by armor. You will want to make sure your shelter is completely sealed, however, because they can shoot through gaps. Skeletons also burn up in daylight.

Skeletons have two very useful drops when killed: Bones and Arrows. Bones can be turned into Bonemeal for use in farming, and picking up Arrows from Skeletons is a lot easier than crafting them.

Zombie

Another of the most common mobs, Zombies wander around the Overworld at night looking for you and your fleshy friends so they can feed on you. Zombies in the PC version attack in swarms, but this has yet to be implemented for the Xbox (it may in the future).

Zombies attack by touching you, and they can quickly take your health down if they trap you in a small area. The main reason for killing Zombies, other than survival, is that they drop Rotten Flesh. This stuff can be eaten by your character in an emergency (4 food units, 80% chance of poisoning), but its main use is to feed tame Wolves.

Like many mobs, Zombies burn during daylight.

Enderman

From the deep, dark lands of The End, the Endermen come to the Overworld to shift blocks around, look awesome and punch you for looking at them. No joke. Endermen are special mobs that aren't hostile to start, but if you're within 64 blocks and your crosshair points at an Enderman above their legs, they will come at you.

Endermen have a pretty tough attack, which is made worse by their ability to teleport around. This also means they can show up almost anywhere, though they tend to avoid sunlight, rain and water. Sunlight, rain, water and fire make them neutral, and any contact with water damages an Enderman—useful tips for combat. It's suggested to attack the legs as well, as the Enderman can't teleport when taking leg damage.

Fighting an Enderman can be necessary when attempting to go to The End, because finding the necessary Ender Pearls otherwise can be very difficult.

Cave Spider

You won't run into Cave Spiders very often, as they only spawn in Abandoned Mineshafts from Monster Spawners, but they're much tougher than regular Spiders. To deal with Cave Spiders, you'll have to fight your way to their spawner and either break it or disable it.

Doing that is more than likely going to mean a bite or two from a Cave Spider, and since they're poisonous, you'll want to bring some Milk to counteract the effects.

Silverfish

Silverfish hang out in fake blocks called Monster Eggs in Strongholds and in caves in the Extreme Hills Biome. The Silverfish can make a Monster Egg out of a Cobblestone, Stone or Stone Brick block, and you can tell it's a Monster Egg by it taking longer than normal to break with a tool or quicker without one.

Breaking a Monster Egg releases a hostile Silverfish, and if it is attacked and not killed, it will wake every Silverfish in a 21x11x21 block radius and make them attack as well. Silverfish do damage every time you make a change on the Y axis (vertical) in relation to the Silverfish. You also hop every time you're damaged, which is a change on the Y axis, so Silverfish can do damage quickly.

Slime

Only spawning below level 40, Slimes have three sizes. When the Slime is killed, it splits into 2-4 more Slimes of the next smallest size until it is made Tiny and killed again.

Slimes are great for experience and are further useful for their drop, Slimeballs, which are used to make Sticky Pistons and Magma Cream. They are also one of the few hostile mobs that can survive sunlight.

Ghast

The scourges of the Nether, Ghasts are huge and shoot at you with explosive fireballs from up to 100 blocks away. These fireballs do 17 damage at close range (8.5 hearts), but they also light the area around on fire, which deals more damage.

To defeat Ghasts, you'll need to build shelters that protect you from their line of site, and hit the Ghast fireballs away with your hand or item. Ghasts drop Gunpowder like Creepers as well as Ghast Tears, a potion ingredient.

Magma Cube

Similar to Slimes, Magma Cubes are hopping creatures found in the Nether that also split into smaller Magma Cubes. The main differences, besides their appearance, is that they can survive falls, lava and water, jump 4 blocks high and do more damage than a Slime.

As with Slime, Magma Cubes are great for experience, and they also drop Magma Cream, another potion ingredient.

Blaze

If you're looking for Blaze Powder, you'll need to find a Blaze, and these tough mobs only show up in Nether Forts. There, Blazes will start popping out once you're within 16 blocks of a Blaze Spawner and can spawn 1-4 at a time, meaning they will build in numbers quickly.

The best method for defeating Blazes is to kill those spawned by using weapons and Snowballs (which do 3 damage to the Blaze). While doing so, destroy or disable the Monster Spawner to avoid more. Snow Golems are also good against Blazes, but will melt in the Nether.

Blazes carry two rare items: Blaze Rods (used in creating Brewing Stands and Blaze Powder) and Glowstone Dust (used in brewing and making Glowstone). Since Blaze Powder is necessary to make an Eye of Ender (among other things), which you need to get to The End, many players find themselves needing to hunt Blazes at some point.

Ender Dragon

There's no greater foe in Minecraft than the Ender Dragon, and there are few greater challenges. Located in The End, the Ender Dragon has 200 health points and does huge damage in the Xbox 360 version (the PC version has different attacks).

The Ender Dragon also gains health by having it beamed from a circle of Obsidian pillars that have Ender Crystals on the top. These will need to be destroyed before you can kill the Ender Dragon, either by shooting them with Arrows or (in the case of the caged Crystals) building to them and breaking them.

It's recommended to take enchanted Diamond weapons and armor and a lot of Obsidian to build with (it won't blow up like most blocks) to defeat the mighty Ender Dragon. Once you do, you'll be rewarded with 12,000 experience (enough to get you to level 78) and the infamous End Poem.

peaceful mobs

Friend/Foe	Found	Health	Exp.	Drop	Follows (when in hand)
SHEEP	Overworld	8 (4 Hearts)	1-3	Wool (1, 1-3 if dropped)	Wheat
CHICKEN	Overworld	4 (2 Hearts)	1-3	Feathers (0-2) Raw Chicken (1) Cooked Chicken (1 if killed by fire) Egg (1 every 5-10 minutes if alive)	Any seed
COW	Overworld	10 (5 Hearts)	1-3	Leather (0-2) Raw Beef (1-3) Steak (1-3 if killed by fire) Milk (when Bucket is used on it)	Wheat
MOOSHROOM	Overworld (Mushroom Biome)	10 (5 Hearts)	1-3	Leather (0-2) Raw Beef (1-3) Steak (1-3 if killed by fire) Milk (when Bucket is used on it) Mushroom Stew (when Bowl is used on it) Red Mushroom (5 when sheared)	Wheat
PIG	Overworld	10 (5 Hearts)	1-3	Raw Porkchop (1-3) Cooked Porkchop (1-3 if killed by fire)	Wheat

Friend/Foe	Found	Health	Attack	Exp.	Drop	Follows (when in hand)
WOLF	Overworld (spawns on grass)	Wild: 8 (4 Hearts) Tamed: 20 (10)	Wild: 2 (1 Heart) Tamed: 4	1-3	None	Bone

Friend/Foe	Found	Health	Exp.	Drop
SQUID	Overworld (Water, spawns between levels 46-62)	10 (5 Hearts)	1-3	Ink Sac (1-3)
VILLAGER	Overworld (Villages)	20 (10 Hearts)	0	Nothing

Friend/Foe	Found	Health	Armor	Attack	Exp.	Drop
ZOMBIE PIGMAN	The Nether, rarely in the Overworld	20 (10 Hearts)	2	Easy: 5 Normal: 9 Hard: 13	5	Rotten Flesh (0-1)

Friend/Foe	Found	Health	Attack	Exp.	Drop
SNOW GOLEM	Created	4 (2 Hearts)	0 (only pushes most mobs) 3 (Blazes only) 1 (Ender Dragon)	0	Snowball (0-15)

hostile mobs

Friend/Foe	Found	Spawns	Health	Attack	Exp.	Drop
CREEPER	Overworld or Nether	Light Level: 7 or less	20 (10 Hearts)	Depends on how close, Maximum: 49 (24.5 hearts)	5	Gunpowder (0-2 when killed but not exploded) Music Disc (when killed by an arrow from a Skeleton)
SPIDER	Overworld	Light Level: 7 or Less, But Can Survive in Light (goes Peaceful)	16 (8 Hearts)	Easy: 2 Normal: 2 Hard: 3	5	String (0-2) Spider Eye (0-1
SPIDER JOCKEY	Overworld	Light Level: 7 or Less, But Can Survive in Light (goes Peaceful)	Spider: 16 (8 Hearts) Skeleton: 20 (10)	Spider-Easy: 2 Normal: 2 Hard: 3 Skeleton-Easy: 2	5 for each	Spider: String (0-2) Spider Eye (0-1) Skeleton: Bone (0-2) Arrow (0-2)
SKELETON	Overworld or Nether	Light Level: 7 or less	20 (10 Hearts)	Easy: 2 Normal: 3-4 Hard: 4-6	5	Arrow (0-2) Bone (0-2)

Friend/Foe	Found	Spawns	Armor	Health	Attack	Exp.	Drop
ZOMBIE	Overworld or Nether	Light Level: 7 or Less	2	20 (10 Hearts)	Around 4	5	Rotten Flesh

Friend/Foe	Found	Spawns	Health	Attack	Exp.	Drop
ENDERMAN	Overworld or The End	Light Level: 7 or Less	40 (20 Hearts)	Easy: 4 Normal: 7 Hard: 10	5	Ender Pearl (0-1)
CAVE SPIDER	Overworld (Abandoned Mineshafts)	From Monster Spawner in Mineshaft Only	12 (6 Hearts)	Easy: 2 Normal: 2 (Poisoned) Hard: 3 (Poisoned) Poison Damage: 1 Every 1.5 seconds Normal: 7 Seconds Hard: 15 Seconds	5	String (0-2) Spider Eye (0-1)

hostile mobs

Friend/Foe	Found	Spawns	Health	Attack	Exp.	Drop
SILVERFISH	Overworld (Strongholds and Rarely Underground in Extreme Hills Biomes)	From Monster Spawner (Strongholds) or Monster Egg (Fake Blocks, Strongholds and Extreme Hills Biomes)	8 (4 Hearts)	1	5	None
SLIME	Overworld	Below Level 40	Big: 16 (8 Hearts) Small: 4 (2) Tiny: 1 (0)	Big: 4 Small: 2 Tiny: 0	Big: 4 Small: 2 Tiny: 1	Slimeball (0-2, only from Tiny Slime)
GHAST	The Nether	Anywhere with space except in Nether Fortresses	10 (5 Hearts)	More the closer it gets, Max of 17	5	Gunpowder (0-2) Ghast Tear (0-1)

Friend/Foe	Found	Spawns	Armor	Health	Attack	Exp.	Drop
MAGMA CUBE	The Nether	Anywhere, often near Nether Fortresses	Big: 12 Small: 6 Tiny: 3	Big: 16 (8 Hearts) Small: 4 (2) Tiny: 1 (1/2)	Big: 6 Small: 4 Tiny: 3	5	Magma Cream (0-1, only Big and Small)

Friend/Foe	Found	Spawns	Health	Attack	Exp.	Drop
BLAZE	The Nether (Nether Fortresses)	Light Level 11 or Less or Monster Spawners, both in Nether Fortresses	20 (10 Hearts)	Fireball- Easy: 3 Normal: 5 Hard: 7 Contact- Easy: 4 Normal: 6 Hard: 9	10	Blaze Rod (0-1) Glowstone (0-2)
ENDER DRAGON	The End	In The End	200 (100 Hearts)	Fireball: Unknown, similar to Ghast Acid Spray: Unknown, very strong	12,000	Nothing

example gallery

We've spent quite a lot of time in this guide telling you how to be a Minecrafter, but we haven't had a lot of space to show you what you can do once you become an expert at the game. So, we're gonna do that right now!

These are some of our favorite creations ever to grace the world of Minecraft, and they span from the simple house to the ground-covering city to complex Redstone circuitry and more. Far from being a comprehensive list of the best Minecraft creations around, these are just some to inspire you to your own creative heights, though we'd be hard pressed to find some better than a few of these bad boys.

Note: Since this guide is based on the Xbox 360 version of Minecraft, we've mostly avoided creations from heavily modded PC versions of the game. But we've thrown in a few that were just too good to resist.

Houses
Your basic Minecraft structure, the house is a traditional creation for most Crafters, whether a newcomer or a veteran to the game.

Not all houses have to be enormous and grand to have great design. This particular house is one of many based on architect Frank Lloyd Wright's famous Falling Water home. The clean design of modern architecture fits perfectly with the straight lines of Minecraft.

But just because it works for modern architecture doesn't mean that Minecraft isn't awesome for more old-school styles as well. This island home by Minecrafter Arcchen is a perfect example of the unique looks that players can create when they set their minds to it.

Buildings

Different from houses, buildings are less about livable space and more about looking awesome. And it won't surprise those of you who have played the game a bit that a few Minecrafters out there have gone above and beyond to create some amazing edifices.

This is actually just one part of a massive world called Sanacraft by creator Tom Yona, but we liked this building so much, we gave it its own page. Of the many, many clock towers created in Minecraft, this is our favorite for its open design that reveals the mechanics of the piece.

When it comes to overall planning, this wondrous structure known as the Cathedral of Artium by Creolucis takes the cake. The aesthetic flair, decorative touches and mirroring of real-life architectural ideas is breathtaking, as is the use of nature in the work.

Screenshot: Minecraft® ™ & © 2009–2013 Mojang/Notch.

Cities

Those of you just starting on your first shelter might be shocked to know that some people out there have created entire cities in the world of Minecraft. Because these are so darn cool, and there's so many styles of cities out there, we're gonna give you five of the best we've seen.

Taking the traditional city structure and giving it a fun flip, these two cities are the definition of Minecrafter imagination. The colors of the first are stunning (Note: it's definitely using a mod), and we can't even imagine the amount of time it would take to set so many blocks. The second, while more understated, is a more realistic city, and we dig that it comes complete with a construction crane.

A different take on the city, this one goes deep underground. Created by TheMinecraftForum, the architecture echoes that of the cave around it, and it's a master class in how to use torches and lighting to perfect effect.

We've included these two together so you can see how even a similar idea can come out looking very differently. Minecraft is all about your personal touch, as you can see by these two unique ancient cities.

Redstone

At this point in the guide, you might be getting a sense that we think Redstone is wickedly cool, and these kinds of creations are why. It's a lot of fun to make a door open with a button or a pressure plate, but these Minecrafters have gone far above and beyond the basics.

Take a look at this. Yep, it's a piano. No, we mean it is a piano. It plays notes like a piano, and it can be programmed by the player. To create this insane machine, Crafter FVDisco had to build a massively complex Redstone circuit system, as you can see from the second image.

If you thought the piano was nuts, get this in your brain: someone has built a working basic computer using Redstone. Don't ask us how it works; you literally have to know how to build a computer to pull this one off. Just the fact that it can be done is enough for us, and we salute those brave souls who have created this masterpiece.

Just for Fun

Some creations aren't just about being cool to look at or performing fancy computer science, some are there just to thrill and amuse Minecrafters as they play. When it comes to fun worlds, these guys have had us button mashing away to no end.

Built by player VTEC4CRX, this is just part of a fully working casino that includes a roulette table and slots among other things. Not only that, but players can place bets with Redstone!

At some point, most Minecrafters get lost, but some get lost on purpose. Enter creators like ROGU3 4NK83R, who made this maze and even once offered free Microsoft Points to anyone who could complete it (he didn't expect they could).

Minecrafters love our Notch (more on him in the first parts of this guide), but some people take that love and turn it into some Minecraft glory. In this case, that means an entire theme park called Notchland. This map involves multiple awesome builds, including an Enderman rollercoaster, a working Ferris wheel and a playable "hoop game" section.

After seeing this creation, many of the PC-loving Crafters had to admit that the Xbox version is pretty great too. This is a roller coaster by nuropsych1, and it is perhaps the coolest thing made so far on Xbox 360 Minecraft. No photo can do this one justice: it's truly a thrilling ride, and you're just gonna have to go look it up for yourself.

Screenshot: Minecraft® ™ & © 2009–2013 Mojang/Notch.

Pixel Art

Minecraft is a very pixelated game, which we love. What we love maybe even more is that instead of seeing the pixels as a bad thing, some players have gone so far as to create an entire art form out of it. It's called pixel art, and some people have gone absolutely nuts with it. When you're looking at these, remember that each and every pixel is one block in Minecraft. That makes even the smallest pixel art creation huge, and it further means that the planning of these is downright intense.

Above: The famous Mona Lisa was rebuilt block-by-block. Left: The art styles of different pixel artists can be very different from one artist to the next.

Top: Some Minecrafters have created extremely detailed images that barely look pixilated. This is done by taking pixel art to an extremely large scale and spending a lot of time making sure every block is placed correctly.

Left: The theme park we showed you a few pages ago might be a great tribute to Notch, but few Minecraft creations have ever gone this far, whether Notch related or not. This is a nearly pixel-for-pixel recreation of a photo of Notch done on a massive scale. It was done in multiple vertical layers by Minecrafters ToxicStriker and MrMonkey91, and it stands as one of the triumphs of the game.

Screenshot: Minecraft® ™ & © 2009–2013 Mojang/Notch.

collaborating & multiplayer

Now that you're a Minecraft expert (or on the way, at least), you're probably ready to see what this here game is like when you add in a couple of other players. Minecraft is built for multiplayer, and playing with others can make for an entirely different kind of experience.

Even better, the Xbox version of Minecraft is built to make multiplayer as easy as possible! PC and PE Minecraft require that someone who is playing have a dedicated server set up for the game, and you then have to know the information to access it, but not for Xbox! Xbox actually has two ways to play with friends: splitscreen, or through Xbox Live.

Minecraft splitscreen!

It's the best!

how to start up a multiplayer game

Splitscreen

The Xbox is the first version of Minecraft to support local multiplayer play, and it's a ton of fun, not to mention incredibly easy to set up. All you need to do is start up one of your worlds and then have the second player turn on their controller and press the "Start" button. They'll need to be signed into an account on the Xbox, but this doesn't have to be a live account. Once they push start, the screen will split into two, and they'll be in your world!

Note: If you have an HDTV and your Xbox is plugged in through an HD cable and set to HD settings, you can have up to 4 players on a splitscreen game of Minecraft.

Take on the Nether with a friend

Set your multiplayer options

Xbox Live

Remember the menu after you select a world where it asks you to pick your mode and difficulty? When you load or start a world that you want to make multiplayer, this is the menu you need to look at. To play on Xbox Live, you need to make sure "Online Game" is checked. You can also select "Invite only" or "Allow friends of friends" if you want those restrictions on.

If you want, you can go into your "More Options" menu at this point and turn on "Host Privileges," which gives you as the host the option to fly, go invisible and turn off exhaustion. Take note, however, that this will negate the possibility of getting achievements or going on the leaderboard for this world.

Once you've selected "Online Game," start your game up so you're in the world. Now, all you need to do is press the "Home" button in the center of your controller and scroll to your "Friends" list and open it. Then select a friend that has Minecraft (only people that are online and have the game can join) and select "Invite to Game" on the next menu. Select Minecraft, send the invite, and if your friend accepts, they'll join your game!

Note: You can also do this through the "Party" feature of Xbox Live. Additionally, you can play splitscreen and invite Live friends to play as well. Up to 8 players can play together.

Make sure everyone's on the same page when you multiplay

Everyone should know what's off-limits and what can be changed

set the rules

Before you get too far into a multiplayer game, you should consider setting some world rules. You might not feel like this is important in a game, but consider this scenario: You've spent hours building something in your world, and you're just about to get it right, but you take a break to work on something else. When you do go back, you see that your friend has built on to your creation and you don't like what they did. Even worse, they took it all apart! This kind of thing is common and can cause major tension, so it's a good idea to set the rules of building ahead of time.

Decide the following things, and your game will go much smoother:

1. What is free game to build or destroy? Is anything restricted?

2. Are all items up for grabs, or will each player keep their own separate?

3. Is there any PVP allowed?

4. Are you going to work together, or each do their own thing?

General Multiplayer Tips

Coming up with great plans and ways to play together is what makes Minecraft multiplayer so popular. Whether you go for a vicious cutthroat Survival game or a peaceful, relaxed Creative build, these ideas will help you get the most out of your game.

Minecraft is better together!

Endermen are a lot easier to kill in groups

Plan a big project: With more than one set of virtual hands at your disposal, you can get seriously creative and take on some massive projects. It's a good idea to get everyone together to plan this kind of thing out, so headsets or local play will help out a lot when trying something ambitious.

Split up the work: Give each player a role in what you're doing. You'll find that doing this will be the difference between quick, efficient builds and chaotic, slow builds that often require lots of retouching. Simplify what each person is doing, and watch those creations soar.

Learn something new together: It's pretty much impossible to learn everything there is to know about Minecraft (just look at what some people can do with Redstone), and learning some of the more complex methods and tactics can be hard. Try it together!

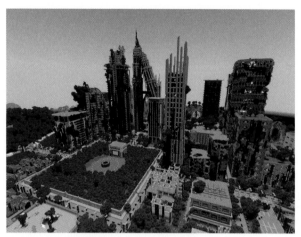

This city definitely took a group to build

Explore with a friend

survival multiplayer tips

Playing a standard game of Survival on multiplayer is enormously fun, primarily because it's no longer just you against the world! You can now do things in half the time, or take on more ambitious projects together.

Give each player a Survival-specific role: For instance, one player could gather Wood and food in the wild, while another could mine for ore and building materials and a third could refine materials, craft items and build on to the shelter. We mention roles again here after we already did because it can make such a huge difference in a Survival game, especially at the beginning.

Provide support when needed: There's nothing worse than getting blown up by a Creeper and having to rush back to all of your stuff, but with another player available, they can always go grab it for you! This is also excellent for combat situations, as two Swords are definitely better than one.

Go exploring: The feeling of accomplishment and wonder that comes from stumbling onto an awesome view or successfully running from a horde of mobs is just that much better when you're with another player. Plus, if you get lost or fall in a hole, you've got someone there to help.

Beat the game: Though the "plot" of Minecraft isn't necessarily the most important part of playing, it's a very cool, very fun thing to play through when you feel like you're ready to take it on. Getting to The End is very difficult and time consuming. It takes a lot of material gathering, not to mention actually fighting the Ender Dragon when you get there. It's highly recommended that you at least fight the Ender Dragon in multiplayer the first time, unless you're a Minecraft combat black belt.

Building something this great takes teamwork

A couple of friends and their homes

creative multiplayer

As you build-lovers know well, Survival certainly isn't the only way to play Minecraft, and neither is it the only way to go about playing multiplayer. With the freedom and safety to build however you like on Creative mode, you'll find adding another player to the mix puts even grander build schemes in your reach.

Make solid plans: We repeat this one for Creative mode because it's pretty likely that you're going to be trying to build some pretty gigantic things in Creative. Because of this, we can't stress enough the helpfulness of even a basic plan for the overall idea, and maybe even for each session of building.

Work to your strengths: Since you've got the freedom to do anything in Creative, that means that people can do what they do best. Say you want to build a giant tower: you're really into architecture and structure-building, but your friend is more of a decorator and your other friend has been dying to try a new Redstone project. Using people that have different strengths and styles together in the game to create your tower will mean that you'll end up with a creation that's strong in multiple areas, instead of just one.

Survival Games

An old fashioned building competition

other ways to play multiplayer

With a game so free-form and open as Minecraft, it was inevitable that players would find other ways to play it together, and boy have they. If you're feeling like something a little different, try one of these great multiplayer alternatives.

1. The Survival Games: Perhaps the most popular game people have created within Minecraft, this involves special maps that have been created for combat. It's based on a popular book/movie with a similar name, and the idea is that a group of players start a game near a bunch of chests filled with items. At a signal, all players rush the items and try to grab as many as they can without getting killed, while also attacking other players. Like said unnamed book/movie, when you die, you're out, and the last player standing wins. There are tons of these maps downloadable online, but you can also try making your own!

2. Building Competitions: Think you can build the best house in 30 minutes? What about 10 minutes? What about on Hard mode in Survival? Building competitions usually involve picking a specific type of creation to build and giving two or more players a deadline in which to do it. This can be on any setting or game type you like, and you can do it with or without a judge. This is one of the most fun challenges in multiplayer, and it not only shows off your skills, it really boosts them!

One fancy maze

Splitscreen makes the competition even fiercer

3. Mazes and Obstacle Courses: Turn Minecraft into a deadly race to the finish by creating or downloading a maze or obstacle course. Add traps, crazy twists and turns and even Redstone puzzles, and maybe leave a prize at the center (some Diamond Armor perhaps?).

4. Capture the Flag: On big games, this can be a whole heap of fun. Create a map with opposing bases, or give each team time to make one, and hide an item designated as a flag within it. Then, have each team try and find the other team's flag while defending their own.

5. All-Out War: Of course, the simplest way to play multiplayer is to just go at each other. You can either set-up ground rules for the contest, or just build and attack! It's a lot of fun, especially when you get creative and use mobs or traps against other players.

6. Get the Most _____: Pick a hard-to-find or craft item, and set a number that a player has to find in Survival to win.

7. Whatever You Come Up With: It's Minecraft, so if you come up with an idea, try it out.

Quick! What do you do in this situation?

top tips

You might have noticed, but there is a ton of stuff to learn about Minecraft. In fact, if you ever find someone who tells you they know every single thing about the game, you've probably got a bit of an exaggerator on your hands. Even the pro-est of the pros always have something new to learn!

In order to get you a head start on some of that pro-knowledge so you can get around to the real crazy stuff in Minecraft, we've put together this little list of pro tips. The rest of this guide has been all about specific sections of the game, but here you'll find more general info that can help you out. Don't let that fool you though: some of these tips are among the most useful in the game. In fact, if we were to suggest just one part of the guide to players looking to take their game to the next level, it'd be this one.

So strap in kiddos, and get familiar with these pro tips and tricks!

DON'T DIG DOWN

Carry a bucket with you

Exploring Tips

You've heard us say it, other people have said it and the game itself will even say it sometimes: never dig straight down or straight up. Straight down can lead to epic falls, possibly into dark areas, and straight up can drop lava or mountains of gravel or sand on your head. Even in Minecraft, lava on the head is usually pretty darn fatal.

Carry water with you in a Bucket whenever possible. Lava can show up out of the blue (sometimes literally, if you find a lava/water meet up), and it's pretty lame to get caught on fire far from home with a bunch of valuable materials on you. Plus, you can always pour the water out and turn lava to Obsidian and walk right over it.

Stuck underwater? Build a small air pocket to breathe! Doors, Trapdoors, Fences and Signs all create air pockets when placed underwater. You can also build a horizontal five block cross shape, then put one block on the block in the center of the cross. Swim under the middle of the cross and break the bottom center block. Voila, a pocket of air!

If you're stuck in a cave or other place underground, and you're tired of trying to get out, dig a diagonal staircase right into the wall. You can also risk digging straight up and placing blocks below you as you go, but there's a good chance you'll have lava, Sand or Gravel fall on your head and kill you if you do.

The ladder-in-water trick will save you from drowning

Build straight up if you need to find your way home

Buckets of Water can be used to climb up or down sheer faces a few steps without falling. You just need to aim it right above (for down) or below (for up) where you'd like to go, then drop the water. Swim up or down the waterfall, then when you get to your destination, turn around and pick the water back up with the Bucket. When going down, make sure you don't pick a place too far away, or you won't be able to pick the water back up. This might not matter in some cases, if you just want off a cliff.

If lost with no Map, build a single-block tower underneath you by jumping and placing blocks below you as you're in the air (Dirt is best). Even better, have another player do it at the same time so you both end up high off the ground where you can see each other. Place torches on the side of the tower if it's night.

Keep a Bed on you so you can sleep if needed wherever you are, but make sure you put it in a safe place.

Carrying a stack of Coal and a stack of Wood is a great way to make sure you always have enough torches. Here's the formula: 1 Wood = 4 Wood Planks = 8 Sticks. 8 Sticks + 8 Coal = 32 Torches. So carrying just 1 Wood and 8 Coal means you can make 32 Torches at any time, or use the materials for other things if needed.

Torches to the right!

Beds just take up one inventory space,
and they can save you a lot of trouble

If you find yourself stuck someplace at night, turn it into a mini-shelter. Make it protected from mobs, light it up with Torches, build a Chest, Crafting Table and Bed if possible and leave a few useful items in the Chest, such as tools, materials and a few Torches. You never know when you'll be back this way.

Exploring areas with walls (caves, Strongholds, the Nether) is much easier when you leave Torches only on one side of the walls as you go in. When you need to find your way out, put the Torches on the other side and follow them to freedom.

There's a trick to finding north without a Compass: put down a block of Cobblestone and look on top for the "L" shape in the pattern. The short side of the "L" always points north, no matter what world you're in or how you place the Cobble down.

Use the right tool for the job—don't use a Diamond Pickaxe on Sand

Lava = ore

Harvesting and Mining Tips

Another common tip: use the right tool for the job. This isn't just because your task will go faster; using the wrong tool for the job also makes that tool lose durability twice as fast. So, not only are you doing the job slower, you're losing your tools faster.

To get the most Wood from tall trees, leave the bottom block of Wood and take out as many as you can reach above it. Then, stand on the bottom block to reach one more before you break it too. If you still can't reach the top by leaving one block of Wood, stack Dirt on top of the Wood while jumping until you get to the right height, then break the Dirt back up.

Replace trees as you chop them down to keep enough Wood around. All you need to do is find a clear area and throw down a Sapling.

Ores often spawn near lava, so go looking for lava to find them. You can use a single bucket of water to turn an entire lava deposit into Obsidian piece by piece as you mine, and you can then mine all around the lava.

You can reach four blocks ahead of you and three blocks down without moving. The most efficient mining method is to point at a single direction and hold down the mining or harvesting button and mine blocks in a row. Because of this, it's good to think in groups of multiple blocks in horizontal or vertical lines, and not single blocks randomly.

Save Coal and a trip to the Furnace by killing food animals with a Flint and Steel. You can light them on fire, and they'll drop fully cooked food.

Cactus can make a good moat

Keep them Creepers away from your home!

Shelter Tips

Moats are awesome, but water is difficult to move through and lava will burn up the items of anything that falls in it. Try a Cactus filled moat that has a walkway over it. Or, if you're feeling fancy, build a system that causes water to flow over the cactus moat and down a hole when you push a lever. Make a little gathering room under the hole, and many of the items from killed mobs will flow down through the hole and into your room. Then, just turn the water off!

Don't put off making a bed and sleeping in it. Beginners are pretty good about this, but advanced players often put it off thinking that they'll be fine. And then a Creeper shows up.

Set up shelters in areas you're working extensively. You'll save a lot of time by making a small shelter with the essentials, and then you'll have a second base too!

Make your home as Creeper proof as possible. This means using Cobblestone or better for walls, as it has a much higher chance of resisting Creeper blasts. Also, build at least part of your house so it's inaccessible from the outside, or at least hard to get to.

Soul Sand can save your Boat from wrecking

Creepers and other mobs can and will ride in Minecarts

Transportation/Movement Tips

Boats damage easily, and will break quickly if they keep hitting blocks (it only takes one ice block), but Soul Sand doesn't damage them. Build harbors with Soul Sand to keep your boats around longer.

If you want to ride a Pig, you'll need to find a Saddle, and as of right now those are only in Strongholds in the Xbox version. However, there is no way to control a Pig when you're on one right now, as this requires a Carrot, which is not yet implemented on the Xbox.

Minecarts react differently to Powered Rails if they're occupied by a player or mob. Unoccupied carts will be able to travel a much shorter distance than occupied carts after a Powered Rail. This is due to occupied Minecarts supposedly having greater momentum. Carts with Chests still count as unoccupied carts.

Most mobs can ride in Minecarts, so don't be surprised to see this happen, and be prepared to kill a few now and then.

Jumping while sprinting can make you move faster, but each action done by the player drains your food. If you do this, keep food on you at all times.

Some weapons are better against certain mobs, like Bows with Ghasts

TNT can really mess a player up

Armor and a cake: two important combat items

Combat Tips

Each armor icon (the things that look like Chestplates) indicates an 8% damage reduction from attacks, explosions, lava and cactus. A full set of Diamond armor gets the full amount of armor icons and protects from 80% of attacks, while Iron armor gives 60% protection.

What you eat before battle matters. You want your hunger saturation as high as possible, otherwise you'll get hungry much quicker as you attack and your health won't regenerate. Good choices for pre-fight meals include Cooked Steak and Porkchop and Cake.

Mobs do not take damage if they still glow red from the last attack.

Attacking while in air after jumping and sprinting gives you the best chance for a critical hit.

If you're stuck in a battle you can't win, use the "turtle" strategy. Look down and jump repeatedly while placing blocks under your feet. Soon you'll be high above the battle, but you'll probably get bored pretty quickly! **In PVP, try unique strategies such as "Finn Fu," which involves creating a wall of flame with a Flint and Steel and hiding a lit block of TNT behind it. Then, run so the player chases you past the wall as the TNT goes off. There are tons of strategies like this online, so go check a few out if you're going to be in heavy combat.**

factoids

- The Minecraft world is rendered in "chunks" of blocks. For the PC, these are 16x16x256 (long x wide x tall). The Xbox version currently goes 128 blocks high, not 256.

- **The Xbox version is currently 864x864x128, with 95,109,632 usable blocks and some that are unusable such as bedrock.**

- The PC version is called "infinite," but it does have a limit of 30,000,000 blocks from the spawn point. After this, things get buggy. The PC version has a total of 60 million x 60 million x 256 blocks, which comes out to a number that reads as 9.216e17.

- **One block in Minecraft is 1 meter x 1 meter x 1 meter, so the surface area of PC Minecraft is 3,600,000,000,000,000 square meters.**

- The surface of the Earth is 510,000,000,000 square meters. That means Minecraft's surface is bigger than the 7058 of the Earth's surfaces put together.

- **To get to the edge of PC Minecraft would take longer than a human lifetime by walking. Players have done it through hacks, and at one point, the game would glitch and create bizarre constructions called the Far Lands and the Stack (at edges and corners, respectively). Now, it creates imaginary blocks and you can't walk into them without it glitching out.**

- There is a website that tracks "world records" in Minecraft that have to be submitted with proof by the user.

- **There are 16 colors of wool in the game**

- Five animals drop food.

- **Notch came in second in 2013's online reader vote for the TIME Magazine 100, a list of the most influential people in the world. Notch had 156,694 votes behind the 173,091 of Egyptian President Mohamed Morsi. Notch had by far the best "Absolutely" to "No Way" ratio of anyone at the top of the poll with 89% saying "Absolutely" and 11% saying "No Way." Notch and Jeb also ended up in the TIME 100 as voted by the magazine's staff.**

- Notch almost called Minecraft "Cave Game".

- **Notch has an old YouTube account under the name "Nizzotch" that's still active. It has over 30 videos, some of which show the early stages of Minecraft's development.**

- The first Minecraft roller coaster was built by Notch. He showed a video of its early tests on YouTube, and it now has over 9 million views.

- **Searching YouTube for Minecraft gets over 80 million results.**

- The Minecraft video with the most views has 105 million. It's called: "Revenge"—A Minecraft Parody of Usher's DJ Got Us Fallin' in Love—Crafted Using Noteblocks.

- **Of the top five Minecraft videos on YouTube, four are parody songs.**

- Like in real life, it's easier to catch fish in the rain in Minecraft.

- **It's said that the Enderman voice is actually people recorded saying "Hey," "Hello" and "What's up?" The recordings were warped and reversed.**

- Minecraft plays a random song at sunrise, noon, sunset and midnight.

- **Each song in Minecraft has a designation in the code and a real-life name, and they were released on a soundtrack in 2011.**

- The music composer for Minecraft is called C418, real name Daniel Rosenfeld.

- **The sounds of the Ghast are actually C418's cat.**

- Minecraft made $240 million in 2012 alone. In all, it's estimated it has made more than $450 million.

other sandbox games

Minecraft is without a doubt the most popular sandbox building game of all time, but it definitely isn't the only such game out there. From the games that inspired Minecraft to games inspired by Minecraft to building games that have nothing to do with our favorite block-based builder, sandbox building is a big and varied genre full of incredibly fun video games. If you're looking for more in the vein of Minecraft, here are the titles to check out.

Terraria is often called the side-scroller Minecraft

Terraria

Like Minecraft, Terraria is an indie game with pixelated graphics that involves digging, fighting monsters and building shelters, but that's about where the similarities end. Very unlike Minecraft, Terraria is not 3D—it's actually a side-scroller (a 2D game that moves to the side like Mario)!

Instead of having players move in any direction, Terraria gives you just four options: Up, down, left or right, and everything in the world is in one of those directions. This might seem like a limitation, but Terraria really makes this system work. The gorgeous pixel graphics and the fact that you have to walk through areas many times lead to a deeper relationship with your environment and the world around your home.

Terraria also differs from Minecraft in its focus. Though you can and indeed must mine and build, the focus of the game is more on its RPG elements such as combat, experience, gaining helpful NPCs and getting better gear. There are tons of different enemies in the game, as well as items and character-based goals to take on. Eventually, players can find themselves in situation like being decked out in Demonite gear in a house with a Dryad and a Wizard about to take on a guy called Doctor Bones.

Another cool feature: Terraria also introduces random events from time to time, such as a Goblin Invasion, which had an army of goblins suddenly show up and attack players' houses. These are unexpected and happen rarely, making for a fun surprise.

Terraria is one of the most accessible games on this list, being available for every major gaming system except the Mac. It's pretty cheap too, so it's definitely one worth checking out.

Dwarf Fortress can be modified to have better visuals

But this is what it looks like in the original

Dwarf Fortress

Here's the thing about Dwarf Fortress: finding a gamer that's heard of Dwarf Fortress isn't super hard, and if you find one that has, there's a pretty good chance that they respect this quirky game. However, finding someone who's actually played Dwarf Fortress is a whole lot harder, and finding someone who's good at Dwarf Fortress…well, let's just say it isn't something that happens to most people in a lifetime.

Dwarf Fortress is one of the inspirations for Minecraft, and it's also one of the hardest video games of all time. On top of that, it's one of the strangest-looking games of all time as well, and its difficulty is largely tied into the way it looks. Dwarf Fortress is what's called an ASCII game, ASCII being a coding system that uses codes and characters based on the English alphabet. Essentially, it's the symbols your keyboard can make, and those are exactly what every single thing in Dwarf Fortress is made from.

That might not seem too complex, until you understand that there are hundreds of different creatures, characters, environments, objects, plants, structures and more in Dwarf Fortress, each of which is represented only by ASCII characters (so keyboard characters).

A gorgeous dwarf-filled fortress

Another visual mod for the game

It's partly what's called a "roguelike" game, which basically means that you control characters in a randomly generated world in which death is just one of many possible events. In Dwarf Fortress' case, this is especially true, as the game generates an entire world, including continents and a huge variety of terrain and environment types.

Your goal in Dwarf Fortress is straightforward: take control of a group of dwarves and try to help them thrive and survive. You do this by giving dwarves tasks, such as mining, cooking or building a mountain fortress. As we mentioned, Dwarf Fortress is one of the most complex games ever, so the list of things your dwarves can do or that can happen is enormous, as are the mind-boggling backstories and histories of each randomly generated game.

Be warned: Dwarf Fortress makes no pretention to of players being even remotely capable of keeping their fort alive and prospering forever. There's no way to "beat" Dwarf Fortress, and in fact the motto of the game is "Losing is fun."

Your dwarves will die, and you will lose in Dwarf Fortress

But that's okay

Because losing is fun!

What they mean by that is that Dwarf Fortress is more about actually telling a new story instead of playing through the same one everyone else does. Because there's so much to do and such a big world full of things to interact with, the possibilities of the game are endless and surprising. You can play through a hundred games in Dwarf Fortress never seeing a dragon, and then one could fly down from a distant mountain and wreck your entire fortress in minutes. You could become partners with a nearby town of elves, or you could smash them to bits.

As a quirky, difficult masterpiece, we recommend that any gamer who has a chance to play Dwarf Fortress give it a shot and see if you can't bring those little dwarves under your control.

Apparently some Infiniminer doesn't like metal

It's easy to see how this game influenced Minecraft

Infiniminer uses a class system, unlike Minecraft

Infiniminer

Another Minecraft inspiration, Infiniminer is where Minecraft got its use of blocks and the idea of mining resources and building things with them. Unfortunately, the source code for Infiniminer was leaked soon after its creation, and people started making their own versions and mods for the game. This made it impossible for the creator to keep updating it, so development was quickly stopped.

Because it's very similar to Minecraft, there's not a whole lot to say about Infiniminer, but we mention it as a nod to those that paved the way for our favorite game. If you feel like playing a bit of gaming history, you can still get the files from the Zachtronics Industries website.

Cube World features gorgeous landscapes...

...full of plenty to do...

...epic combat and much, much more.

Cube World

If you always wished that Minecraft had more RPG elements to it, such as classes, races, spells, more weapons and extended combat, you'll wanna check out Cube World. Cube World is a block-based fantasy adventure game that puts the focus on killing monsters and exploring in order to find more monsters to slay.

Cube World resembles Minecraft in that it uses blocks to create everything and terrain is destroyable, but the building function isn't done yet, so there's no house creation. What is there is a gorgeous game, admittedly prettier than Minecraft, which has absolutely tons to do in terms of role playing, adventuring and bad-guy slaying. It looks and feels a little like later Zelda games if Zelda was set in a Minecraft-like world. Of the sandbox builders in progress, this is one of the best put-together.

Minecraft meets the FPS!

Ace of Spades lets you blow people up *and* build

This is one of the more popular games that took a nod from Minecraft

Ace of Spades

If Cube World is Minecraft-meets-Zelda, Ace of Spades is Minecraft meets the online first person shooter. It combines the idea of building and digging in a block-based world with typical FPS combat matches, such as "capture the flag," "team deathmatch" and defensive modes.

Like most FPS games, Ace of Spades has a class system and multiple weapon choices, but deciding which class and items you carry also depends on whether or not you plan on building or mining. The idea is that some players will create forts and other defenses for their team while helping out with the combat when they can, while others focus more on killing. Additionally, mining can be used offensively to take down or sneak into enemy bases.

Maps on Ace of Spades can be randomly generated or player-created, and they look great, usually complete with epic terrain and nicely built structures and cities. Ace of Spades is a very, very different experience from Minecraft and most other block builders despite its similarities, making it one of the most notable Minecraft-related games out there.

StarMade

Honorable Mentions

These are some block-building sandboxers that we didn't have space to talk about, but are absolutely worth checking out:

• FortressCraft
• Blockland
• Mythruna
• Voxel.js
• Planet Explorers
• Aetherius
• Blockscape
• Roblox
• Eden World Builder
• Manic Digger
• Kogama
• StarMade

Voxel.js

Planet Explorers

The Sims

SimCity 2

Roller Coaster Tycoon

Evil Genius

Dungeon Keeper

Non Block-Based Sandbox Games

The term "sandbox game" didn't come about when block-builders did; it's actually been around for quite some time, and it refers to a huge number of different games. Many of these games are builders, while others are entirely about the action or RPG elements. In reality, "sandbox" simply refers to the fact that the world of the game is open and the player can (for the most part) choose what they do, and the world around the player changes or reacts to their choices.

Here's a quick list of a few other sandbox games (or games with sandbox modes) to compare and contrast with Minecraft and the block-building games. These are definitely not all of the sandbox games out there, but they're some great examples of the genre.

Builders:
- The Sims series
- SimCity (and the other Sim games)
- Dungeon Keeper
- The Caesar series
- Evil Genius
- RollerCoaster Tycoon (and the other Tycoon games)

Skyrim

Animal Crossing

Baldur's Gate II

Bully

RPGs:

- The Elder Scrolls series
  (Skyrim, Oblivion, Morrowind, Daggerfall etc.),
- The Animal Crossing and Harvest Moon series'
- The Fallout series
- Bioware's Forgotten Realms games
  (Baldur's Gate I & II, Icewind Dale etc.),
- Bully

Assasin's Creed

Grand Theft Auto

Batman: Arkham City

Project Zomboid

Action/Adventure:
- The Grand Theft Auto series
- The Assassin's Creed series
- Garry's Mod
- S.T.A.L.K.E.R.
- Dead Rising
- Dead Island
- Batman: Arkham City
- Project Zomboid
- Shenmue

ADVANCED
MINECRAFT

Introduction

MINECRAFT! It's everywhere these days, and we here at the Minecrafter absolutely love it. If you hadn't heard of this game before last year, you probably have now, as Minecraft has absolutely exploded onto the public consciousness like few games ever have. Minecraft truly is the king of all indie games, and as one of the most successful and profitable pieces of entertainment ever created, more and more fans are flocking to our favorite blocky builder game all the time. Nowadays it seems just about everyone's getting their mine on!

Because of that overwhelming demand for more!more!more! Minecraft, folks everywhere are looking to learn more about this simple-seeming, but actually extremely complex game. And that, dear Crafters, is where Minecrafter Volume 2 comes in.

Where the first issue of Minecrafter took Crafters from their first steps in the world of the game to basic Redstone and structure building, this jam-packed second issue focuses on more advanced topics and concepts and goes deeper into specific strategies. Want to know how to Kill More Mobs? That's in here. Looking to get a start on a Redstone computer? This guide will put you on the right path. Want to "beat" the game and be the first on your block to read the End Poem without using the Internet? You're about to slay you an Ender Dragon, kiddo!

We've also thrown in more info on the culture of the game outside of actual play in this issue, such as more about Notch and Mojang, Minecon and the various communities that have built up around the game. As Minecraft has grown in popularity, we've started to see some seriously cool stuff go down surrounding the game, and we've collected some excellent data and striking shots to get you up to speed.

Minecrafter Vol. 2 is all about taking you beyond the start of your Minecraft journey and deeper into the game you love (or will soon!). From those who want to build higher, bigger and better, to those who are looking to "beat" this most unconventional of games, to those wanting the newest Redstone tips and tricks, Minecrafter Vol. 2 is your go-to guide for the best strategies, the coolest new structures and every-darn-thing Minecraft there is.

There's a world of infinite imagination and excitement waiting for you just on the other side of this page, so as we say here at the 'Crafter, grab your pickaxe and let's dig in!

State of Minecraft

Before we dive into those tasty, tasty strategies you came to this book for, let's take a moment and look at the state of the Minecraft phenomenon and where it has come in the last year.

{ **12 million** new copies downloaded in just three years! }

Biggest Year Yet

It's not often that a video game (or anything for that matter) reaches its greatest successes yet nearly five years after originally coming out, but that's exactly what has happened for Minecraft! 2013 was truly Minecraft's year, as not only did the fan-base absolutely explode, but the game itself became much more complex, and there were even two entirely new versions of the game released for the Raspberry Pi and the PlayStation 3!

Speaking of the fans, just take a look at these numbers: It took the PC version of Minecraft from 2009 until January 2011 to be downloaded 1 million times, but as of 2014, the computer version of this much-loved game has now seen an absolutely stunning *13*

To begin with, Mojang and 4J (the makers of the console ports for the game) have stated that not only will Minecraft continue to be updated for the Xbox and PS3, but that a version will also be released for the new PS4 and Xbox One systems! These versions are said to be compatible with the previous version for each system, meaning players should soon be able to move their Xbox 360 and PS3 worlds onto the newest, most powerful gaming systems on the market.

million downloads. That's **12 million** new copies downloaded in just three years! The Pocket Edition and Xbox 360 version have equally impressive numbers, with the PE earning 10 million downloads (calculated May 2013) and the Xbox version having been purchased a cool 8 million times (August 2013). Considering that these numbers don't even include the brand-spankin' new PS3 version or the Pi version, not to mention the months since May and August (for the PE and Xbox, respectively), the number of official copies of Minecraft out there is estimated to be over 40 million as of the start of 2014, making it one of the biggest entertainment titles in history.

What to Expect Next

As we've mentioned, this book deals primarily with the two fastest-growing versions of Minecraft (the console and Pocket Editions), and boy-oh-boy is there a lot of new stuff that is set to come out soon for both platforms!

For the PE (Pocket Edition), it's been hinted that an official, working multiplayer version is soon to be released, and we can only hope that such an update will also bring the PE closer to the console, adding more materials, mobs and features.

On the console side, we've already seen one major update since the last Minecrafter, and that added such awesome new features as the Jungle Biome, the fearsome Iron Golem, the adorable Ocelot and new events like Villager breeding and Zombie raids. This may seem like a lot, and it definitely has made the game even more interesting, but it seems that the best is yet to come for the console versions.

Two New Platforms to Craft on in 2014

If 2013 was Minecraft's biggest year so far, 2014 looks like it just might rival that title in a big way.

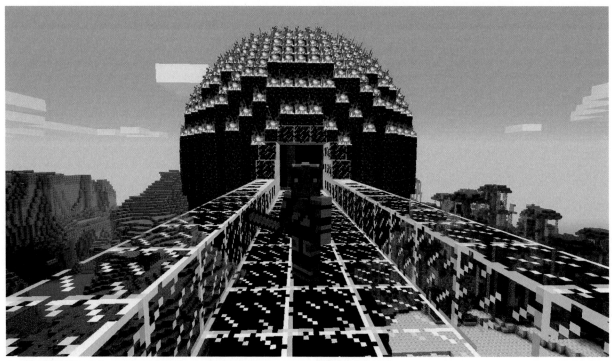

Crafter DE4DI3AVES was one of the many to join the game in the last two years

Stained Glass is one thing we expect to see on the console

Among the rumored additions in the upcoming TU14 update for the console are the long-awaited Horses (you can ride 'em!), Withers, Anvils and Hoppers, with some hopeful Minecrafters saying that there's a chance we might see Emerald Ore, Ender Chests, Temples and even trading with Villagers added in. These have all been in the PC version for some time now, and we should see at least a few (if not all of them) on the console in upcoming months.

Speaking of the PC, while this book isn't specifically about that version of the game, we can learn a lot about what's to come for the PE and console versions by looking at what has come out for PC. 2013 saw one of the biggest updates yet to any version of Minecraft with version 1.7.2 for the PC (October). With an absolutely massive amount of new content, including new Mobs, new Biomes and tons of new materials (Stained Glass!), not to mention the

Crafters Sadie and Chloe built this neat blimp in Minecraft PE

awesome new Amplified world type (ravines that go all the way down to the Bedrock!), this update was called The Update that Changed the World, and it shows us that over the next year or so we should continue to get huge amounts of new content added to the other versions of the game.

Where We're At

With all of this (and who knows what else) in store for us from the folks at Mojang, and with Minecraft expanding to just about every major platform out there, this is the most exciting time yet in the world of Minecraft! For you new folks, welcome to one of the most exciting phenomenons and communities in entertainment, while for you veteran Crafters, let's get to work and make even bigger, even better builds. As they say, the sky's the limit in Minecraft.

Cats and Ocelots are some of the most recent additions to the console version of Minecraft

A pair of towers sits atop an Extreme Hills Biome.

What Exactly Do We Mean by "Biome?"

This might seem like an easy question to answer, and in a basic sense, the definition of "Biome" in Minecraft is pretty straightforward: Biomes are the different types of land you can find in Minecraft. However, there are actually two distinct types of Biomes that can be found in the game. For this book, we'll call them "Area Biomes" and "Feature Biomes," respectively, and you'll notice when you play that you'll often find them existing together, with the Feature Biome set within the larger Area Biome.

Area Biomes: We use this term in Minecrafter to refer to the large sections of land that contain certain plants, mobs and aesthetics (for instance, Desert Biomes are mostly yellow and tan with little life, while the Jungle Biome is lush with life and is full of deep greens and browns). When running around the world of Minecraft, Area

Biomes are what you'll most often be in when above ground, and the border between one Area Biome and the next is usually pretty easy to see, as the ground will change color from one Biome to the next. Think of Area Biomes as different types of nature, or environments.

Feature Biomes: Where Area Biomes refer to areas where certain plants and mobs live, Feature Biomes are more recognizable by their shape. Think of them as natural structures, including Beaches, Rivers, Ravines and Hills. Caves aren't technically considered a Biome, but we've included them with Feature Biomes as they have many similarities.

Why You Should Know Your Biomes

Other than the obvious reason that you want to be an ultra-level, super-guru, Minecrafter genius-person, there is an important practical reason that knowing your various Biomes is a great idea: some items, mobs, structures and even Feature Biomes exist mostly or even exclusively in specific Biomes.

For instance, say you're looking for a lot of Wood and you need it really quickly. Well, if you know your Biomes, you know to stay away from the Desert Biome, and hopefully there's a Jungle Biome nearby. Ready to go cave-diving? The Extreme Hills Biome is your best bet, and you're unlikely to find what you're looking for in the Jungle.

The fact that not all Biomes are created equal, and that some contain resources you'll need more often (like Wood) and others don't, also makes it important to know Biomes at the beginning of your game when choosing a spot for a home. There's nothing worse than building a super-sweet house and then realizing that you'll have to hoof it about five minutes to the north to get more Wood because you built your home in a Biome without many trees.

The Biome Breakdown

So now that you know why you'll be an even better Crafter when you get your Biome game on lock-down, let's get into it! While we're not going to get into the crazy math that goes behind each Biome (it's out there online, if you're interested), we are going to give you a basic idea of what each Biome is like, what you can find there, why you might want to visit it and whether or not it's a good spot to build a base. We've simplified the info for the Feature Biomes, as they are more about looks and things don't spawn exclusively in them.

Area Biomes

Plains Biome: What It's Like- One of the more common Biomes, the Plains (or Grasslands) is full of Grass, Flowers and some smaller Trees. It usually features plenty of mobs (both hostile and friendly) roaming about, and you can sometimes find caves, lakes, Villages and Lava pools scattered around it.
Unique Items, Resources and Mobs: None

Reasons to Visit: It's peaceful and has plentiful Grass (for Seeds) and peaceful mobs to hunt. It's also good for later in the game when you have a lot of resources and want a big space to build something in.

Good for a Base? Only on the edges. Building too far into the Plains will lead to lots of time spent running to Forest Biomes and others with more resources, but building on the edges of the Plains can be fun.

Forest Biome

What It's Like: Trees, Trees and more Trees! Another very common Biome, the Forest Biome is one of the most useful early in the game, as they provide large amounts of Wood.

Unique Items, Resources and Mobs:
- Wolves are often found wandering outside of Forest Biomes, but they tend to spawn here.

- Though you can find plenty of Trees elsewhere, the Jungle Biome is the only Biome with a greater concentration of Trees (and those are almost exclusively Jungle Trees).

Reasons to Visit: You need Wood! Also, they are excellent for mob hunting, even in the day, as the shadows created by Trees are ideal for keeping hostile mobs spawned.

Good for a Base? Absolutely! The easy access to wood makes Forests great for your first base, though you might want to find an edge of the Forest so that you don't have to clear out so many leaves.

Desert Biome

What It's Like: Sparse of life and resources, the Desert is pretty cool-looking, but is not a great place to spend large amounts of time unless it is near another, more resource-heavy Biome.

Unique Items, Resources and Mobs:
- Cactus grows in the Desert and can be used for traps and decoration.

- Sand and Sandstone, while not exclusive to the Desert, will be found in the largest amounts here.

- Dry Bushes also grow here and are mostly used for decoration.

Reasons to Visit: The three primary reasons people head to the Desert are Sand, Cactus and Desert Villages. For whatever reason, Villagers love the Desert, and you'll often find a Village or two within. Primarily, however, Deserts are best for grabbing Sand for making Glass and Sandstone.

Good for a Base? Only at the edge of the Desert and another Biome. It's good to have a Desert near your base (as you'll probably want Glass at some point), but its utter lack of trees is a huge drawback for building a base there.

Swamp Biome

What It's Like: Lots of little bits of land surrounded by water. Features short Oak Trees covered in Vines, often has Mushrooms and Lily Pads around.

Unique Items, Resources and Mobs:
• Lily Pads are most commonly found here. These are fun decorations, but you can also build bridges across water with them.

Reasons to Visit: Swamps are okay for Wood, but you're always better off finding a Forest Biome when you need large amounts. Most of the reason players go to Swamps is to find the resources that are common there, such as Lily Pads, Vines and Mushrooms.

Good for a Base? Can be a cool-looking spot for your home, but you'll need to have a Forest nearby in the long-run.

Extreme Hills Biome

What It's Like: You'll know this one when you see it: huge hills with massive cliffs, overhangs and even waterfalls. One of the most interesting-looking Biomes there is, and a fan-favorite.

Unique Items, Resources and Mobs: None as of now (Emerald Ore is exclusive here but not yet included on the console versions of Minecraft).

Reasons to Visit: When looking for caves and resources, this is by far your best bet. Extreme Hills Biomes are absolutely riddled with cave openings, and because there's so much exposed rock, you'll often be able to simply look around outside for Coal and Iron Ore.

Good for a Base? Again, yes, but only if there's a Forest nearby. One trick is to start at a Forest, collecting a lot of Wood and Saplings, and then move to a nearby Extreme Hills Biome to build your home. As they're great for caves, it helps you later in the game, and you can always plant your Saplings on the Extreme Hills (which looks awesome too).

Mushroom Island Biome

What It's Like: Maybe the most unique Biome, this features purple-ish Mycelium as its primary building block and has Huge Mushrooms that look like trees. Always found out in the Ocean Biome.

Unique Items, Resources and Mobs:

- Mycelium, a unique Dirt-like building block that is purple/grey and which Mushrooms like to grow on.

- Mooshrooms hang out on the Mushroom Island. These are Cows that have Mushrooms growing on them. These are great food sources, as you can get Milk, Beef, Mushrooms and Mushroom Stew from them, as well as Leather.

- Giant Mushrooms are another great food source, as chopping them down gives you large amounts of Mushrooms.

Reasons to Visit: For one, there are no hostile mobs on these islands, so they're nice as sanctuaries. They're also very good for food, and if you can manage to get a Mooshroom back to your base, you'll have a constant plentiful food source.

Good for a Base? Nope. You could always build a secondary base on one, or a bridge or tunnel connecting your base to one, but because they are so isolated out in the water, you're going to constantly have to go back to the main landmass to get other resources.

Taiga Biome

What It's Like: Can often be snowy and is a sort-of "Russian"-style forest with Spruce Trees and Wolves.

Unique Items, Resources and Mobs:

- Another great place to find Wolves (though again, they aren't unique to here).

- The best bet for Spruce Trees

Reasons to Visit: Mostly just to chop down Spruce Trees or find Wolves to tame.

Good for a Base? Can be, though you'll be stuck with just one Wood type for the most part. Mostly good for raiding for Spruce Wood.

Jungle Biome

What It's Like: BIIIIIG Trees. Like, really, really big Trees. And lots of them. Tons of foliage in general, and usually some hilly areas and lakes.

Unique Items, Resources and Mobs:

- Jungle Trees. These are absolutely the best Wood resource out there, and you'll love finding a Jungle just to get at these giant Trees. They can be as big as four times wider than a normal Tree and many, many times taller. You'll often find them covered in Vines as well.

- Cocoa Pods are sometimes found on Jungle Trees and are used in food crafting.

- Ocelots! One of the cutest and most useful mobs, the Ocelot is very hard to catch but when tamed they can be used as pets or as guards against Creepers (that's right, Creepers hate Cats and won't go near 'em!)

Reasons to Visit: Get on top of Jungle Tree and chop down all the Wood you'll ever need (well, for about a project or so at least). You'll also want Cats at some point to protect your stuff, so Ocelot taming is a good reason as well.

Good for a Base? Sure! With all that Wood around, why not try a tree-house? You'll probably need to visit others for certain resources, but the Jungle is a great Biome for building, if you can clear out a spot.

Ocean Biome

What It's Like: Lots and lots of water, going off into the distance. There are also underwater caves and Squids!

Unique Items, Resources and Mobs:

- Squids can sometimes find their ways into Rivers, but you're mostly gonna find these neat little guys (that drop Ink Sacs) in the Ocean.

Reasons to Visit: If you're feeling adventurous and want to try an underwater cave, or if you need a Squid. They can also be pretty good for taking a Boat around, as you can explore the coast.

Good for a Base? Not at all. The Ocean has zero Wood and is hard to build in, not to mention breathe. Of course, everyone wants to have an underwater base at some point, so if you've got the resources, it's a fun place for a secondary home later in the game.

Of all the Biomes, the Nether is by far the most dangerous. That also makes it one of the most fun, however!

Nether Biome

What It's Like: Fire, Lava, things trying to kill you constantly, little in the way of food. Basically super, super hostile.

Unique Items, Resources and Mobs: TONS. The Nether is like a whole new world, and most of what you'll find there is exclusive.

- Nether Rack is a red building block that when set on fire stays on fire.

- Nether Brick is made from Nether Rack and has a similar relationship to Stone's relationship to Cobblestone.

- Soul Sand is a building block that makes things move slow, great for docks for your Boat.

- Glowstone is a building block that produces light.

- Nether Wart is a plant resource that is used in recipes and only found in the Nether

- Magma Cubes are like Slimes, but made of fire and Lava and are pretty darn dangerous.

- Ghasts are huge, flying creatures that shoot fireballs and will seriously mess you up.

- Zombie Pigmen are passive, unless you attack them, and they wield weapons.

- Blazes are some of the more dangerous mobs, floating around and shooting Fire Charges at you. You'll need to kill some at some point if you want to make it to The End.

Reasons to Visit: Besides all of the unique resources, the mobs and the unique things they drop, you'll need to get to the Nether to get items you need to get to The End.

Good for a Base? You can try, but Beds explode on placement in the Nether, so don't expect to get too comfy. Take Stone and Cobblestone with you, as you're going to need something to protect you from Ghast blasts.

Feature Biomes

River Biome

What It's Like: Neat little rivers, cutting through the land and giving it definition.

Reasons to Visit: They look very cool, and it's always fun to build near one.

Hills Biome

What It's Like: Just plain ole hills, these can occur on many Biomes including Desert, Plains and Forests.

Reasons to Visit: Good for building on top of, as they offer a view of the surrounding mobs at night.

Ravine Biome

What It's Like: Giant gashes cut into the land that go down very, very far. These can be on the surface or underground, and can often contain waterfalls and Lava falls.

Reasons to Visit: They can be neat to build across or on either side of, but mostly they are just spectacular for getting ore and finding caves, as you can just look at the wall and see where the deposits are.

Beach Biome

What It's Like: Little bits of Sand on the edge of water.

Reasons to Visit: Mostly just for Sand, and sometimes they have Clay as well!

Feature Biomes

Cave Biome

What It's Like: Winding, often-complex tunnels through the ground, full of hostile mobs.

Reasons to Visit: These are your best-bet for running into the best resources and structures in the game (like Diamond, Redstone, Fortresses and Abandoned Mineshafts). You'll be spending a lot of time in caves, and it's a good idea to find one very big one and build a little base in it to explore from.

"Snowy" Biomes

What It's Like: Many Biomes have "cold" or "Snowy" versions where you can find Ice and Snow, as well as get actual snow-falling animations. Plains, Taiga, Rivers and Beaches can all have "Snowy" versions.

Reasons to Visit: You can get Snowballs here, which can be turned into Snow Blocks. Ice is also fun to use, as you slip across it, and the "Snowy" Biomes just look plain awesome.

Deep Ocean Biome

What It's Like: The Ocean Biome, except with massive underwater mountains and Ravines.

Reasons to Visit: Same as the Ocean Biome, but good for giant underwater structures.

{ "Infinite power just isn't very interesting, no matter what game you're playing. It's much more fun when you have a limited tool set to use against the odds. Usually, a new player to Minecraft doesn't make it through the first night. They're just not prepared for the danger. It's a harsh lesson but it establishes the rules." }

— Notch on why Minecraft is the way it is

A Jungle Biome sits just above a Cave Biome, giving this area a quite cool look.

Kill More Mobs

Thing is, when you play Minecraft in Survival mode, some creature at some point in the game will attempt to kill you, and it will succeed. We all know this when we start a world (which typically involves dying once or five times), but after a while you get comfy in your safe house and well-lit mine, and you forget that outside your cozy walls lies death. And then it comes for you, in the form of a sizzling Creeper you didn't see until it was too late, or a nest of Cave Spiders that you suddenly crack into, and you're dead. All your gear is probably lost, you're far from where you were, and then you remember: combat happens in Minecraft. **Let's get you ready to fight.**

1. Prepare for Battle, Young Miner

Nothing you do in Minecraft is more important to your success in combat than preparation. Every good strategy involves at least some of it, and it is the core of almost all successful offense and defense. Fail to prepare, or at least think ahead a bit, and you're gonna die. Do even the smallest bit of prep work, and you're gonna kill some mobs, kiddo.

So let's get you prepared. These are far from the only ways to prepare in this game, but they'll at least get you set on the path to tasty triumph over the dark forces that wait outside the walls of your home.

Crafter Robot Noise is decked out in enchanted armor and a Diamond Sword, ready for battle.

You'll notice the difference that Diamond gear makes right away. There really is no substitute.

Eat This, Not That

Best before battle:
- Golden Apple
- Cooked Porkchop
- Steak

Good before battle:
- Cooked Chicken
- Mushroom Stew
- Bread
- Cooked Fish

Bad before battle:
- Apple
- Melon
- Uncooked meat
- Cookie

Light up the area around your base. Hostile mobs only spawn where the light level is low. When you leave your base unlit, you're letting the mobs choose when to fight you. Turn the tables by lighting the area around your base, that way you only fight on your terms.

It's okay to spend on gear. We know, we know— you want to save that Diamond for <insert difficult to acquire item here>. Well, we get that, but trust us on this one. The amount of lesser materials you will save by spending that Iron or Diamond on good Armor and weapons is going to make that enchanted Diamond Sword pay for itself. You won't just die less, you'll die a lot less, and your ability to kill mobs quickly will result in experience and drops galore.

A miner's gotta eat. Food is the most often forgotten and perhaps most important part of combat. Health regeneration and the ability to sprint (and thus knock the mob back, aka "knockback") depend on your continuing to have a full food bar (the bar with the meat-on-bones). Eat foods that have good hunger-to-saturation restoration levels before battle for best effects, and avoid those with low hunger-to-sat. You should also bring such foods with you when going out hunting and eat them whenever hungry. Keeping yourself well-fed with the right foods all throughout your combat period is essential.

Screenshot: Minecraft® ™ & © 2009–2013 Mojang/Notch.

This pit and staircase combo is an excellent build for mob hunting, as it allows you to shoot from on top of it, drawing mobs toward you and hopefully into the pit. Make it even better by building a fence and a gate at the back.

Prepare the land. Make the battlefield your own, not just with lights, but with traps, murder holes and more. The thrill of attacking blind is great at times, but if you're looking to become a true hunter, take the daylight hours to prepare your hunting grounds for maximum success. Create pits, holes and cliffs to lead or knock mobs into and know where they are. Build tunnels and places to attack from above (little towers and forts) that you can access but keep you safe from mobs. This is where you can start to have the most fun with hunting (and essentially farming) mobs, and where you can get the most creative. Turn the area around your base into a place that invites mobs in, murders them brutally and leaves the spoils for you to collect.

2. Offense Is the Best Offense

When combat comes, and it will, don't go swinging blindly. And in fact, don't just swing. The Minecraft community has come up with a few tried and true methods that will amplify your ability to come out of a mob encounter on the life-having end by enormous amounts, and you'll find they'll lead to a lot fewer frantic trips back to your dropped pile of loot.

Sprint and hit to get a knockback. Attacking a mob at sprint causes you to knock it back. This is good for two reasons: It puts distance between you and the mob, and it gives you the opportunity to knock them off of something and damage them. This is especially useful when you know or have prepared the battleground.

Circle around while attacking: the circle strafe. One of Minecraft's two most trusted attack styles, circle strafing involves putting an enemy in the center of your vision while you walk around them in a circle, attacking the whole time. Called the circle strafe, this method makes it hard for most enemies to attack while giving you the opportunity to do damage. NOTE: does not work on Creepers unless you're just crazy good at it.

Flint & Steel

Is, in fact, so useful in combat that it should be considered second most essential to a Sword.

Attack, pull back and draw them in, attack again: kiting. Kiting is the second of the two sacred Minecraft combat strategies. "Kiting a mob" is when you hit a mob and then back away while keeping your vision focused on the mob. Mobs immediately attack after you hit them, so by pulling away, you can direct them toward you (as if you were pulling them on a kite string). As your target comes to attack, time a second attack perfectly so that they are hit and knocked back a bit, giving you the chance to back away again and repeat the process. Kiting is one of the safer and most effective strategies in Minecraft combat, and it can be used in combination with archery as well as with traps for seriously damaging attacks.

• Swords aren't your only weapons. The best hunters use all of their tools. Swords are the primary weapon, but you can also light blocks on fire with Flint and Steel, drop Lava, suffocate with Gravel or Sand (you have to time those just right), drown with Water and even slow mobs down with Cobwebs or Soulsand. Try all of these in combat at least once and arm yourself with the weapons you are best at using.

3. Keeping Alive: Defense in Minecraft

While prepping and attacking correctly are great, sometimes you just need to stay alive to win the fight. And, let's be honest, sometimes you just need to stay alive period. Don't let your first thirty deaths get ya down, Crafters: staying alive can be done, and done well.

Putting a wall between the Crafter and the Creeper will save you over and over.

Putting Torches down while attacking ensures that mobs won't spawn in this exact area again (though they might be able to travel there).

This angry Spider can't get to his attacker when he's underwater!

Use the zigzag method. Most mobs do not do well with direction change when it comes to attacking (the Silverfish being a definite exception). Skeletons in particular just can't handle it, so whether you're attacking or running away, strafing from side to side will boost your chances of success.

Put blocks between you and them. Mobs will chase you, but if you make a move when they can't see you, they won't know you did it. This means that getting behind something and then changing direction or tactics can save your butt more often than not. This is great for attacking, but even better when you need to get yourself out of combat quickly.

Go underwater. No mob can swim to try and kill you underwater, so if you need to get away, dive down, kid.

Spam those torches. Remember, mobs will keep spawning anywhere there is darkness, and if mobs have put you in a bad situation in one spot on the map once, they probably will do so again unless you do something. Spamming torches on the environment when running is a great preventative measure for now and the future.

Any good general will tell you: always take the higher ground when possible.

4. Generally Good Ideas

Just plain smart things to think about when it comes to Minecraft huntin'.

With full health, this Zombie should be no problem. If this Miner was hurtin', however, it would be best to avoid combat in this dark tunnel.

Creepers start their countdown when you are within three blocks and end it when you leave the three block range. That might sound like pretty specific advice, but anyone who's played the game much at all knows that no other mob really compares to the Creeper when it comes to doin' damage. Know this fact and use it to your advantage.

Don't Fight Unless You Can and Want to. You don't have to prove your bravery in Minecraft. Fighting when you are close to death, don't have good gear, are far from home or are otherwise unprepared leads to death, which leads to losing precious items and time. Run away first, fight when the odds are in your favor, and your game will progress a whole lot faster than that of your "brave" friends.

5. Colonel Creeperkiller's Strategy Corner

Okay we made that name up, but this neat little strategy section needed a flashy title. Pulled from the deep depths of the Crafter community, these specific strategies should be learned and used when you find yourself in a tough spot. When you get good at them all and combine them with the above tips, you'll find yourself wrecking your way through wave after endless wave of mobs, reaping their delicious experience orbs and laughing as you stand tall as the apex predator of the Minecraft world. Or something like that. NOTE: These tricks can be used on mobs or, if you're feeling rascally, on other players.

By digging above this Zombie, he has no idea he's about to die.

Getting past mobs in tunnels is a great use of the Ender Pearl (if you can afford to use one).

When a Creeper's coming head-on like this, the best option is to get around him and hit from behind.

The Duck and Swing. Best on mobs, make the mob lose sight of you, then move to attack mode. Basically, move to a place where the mob can't see you. They will continue to come at the last place they saw you, so you can move yourself to a place where you can attack them. Swing around behind or above, and you'll have the advantage on the unsuspecting mob. This strategy is super tricky in PVP, but it feels pretty great when you pull it off.

The Reverse Sapper. Tunnel above enemies or mobs and unleash your fury. Don't feel confined to the way the environment is set up. If you know where they'll be, dig so that you pop up just above them and rock them with attacks. One of the most effective strategies there is.

Ender Bouncing. Pretty straightforward, but expensive: throw Enderpearls to teleport around the battlefield. Especially effective when you throw them through throw walls of fire or where enemies can't see/reach, gaining you a tactical advantage.

A Creeper's about to learn what the Pit Knock is.

The Mini Murder Fort from a distance.

Stack your Mini Murder Fort with some useful items.

Finn Fu done correctly is devastating.

The hilarious Sato Technique about to make a Creeper pay.

The Pit Knock. Set up a pit that's either deep enough to damage anything that falls in it or that has something damaging in it like Cactus or fire. Lure enemies near it and knock 'em in with a sprint attack or a weapon with the Knockback enchantment. Mob falls in, collect loot at the bottom, profit. Can also be made more complicated by creating a drowning or suffocating trap (see the Inventions section).

The Murder Hole. Create a border around a part of your base where you leave one block open just above where the ground level is on the outside of the base. On the inside of the base, make this spot accessible so that it is at your head-height. This will make it so you can attack the feet of mobs, while most can't get to you. Spiders, however, still sometimes can. Stinkin' Spiders.

The Mini Murder Fort. Get yourself all geared up and find a good spot out in the wild during the day where mobs are likely to spawn at night. Build yourself a little spot where you can reach mobs on all sides but they have a hard time getting to you. This can either be slightly up in the air or slightly underground (or both, for The Ultra Mini Murder Fort), putting you just out of reach of most mobs. Wait til dark, and then wreck all that dare come near. Even Spiders will usually just jump on top, and if you have a one-block hole punched in the ceiling, you'll have a fine window to kill them through.

Finn Fu. Start a ranged attack on an enemy with a Bow, then create a large firewall on a line of blocks in front of you using Flint and Steel. The enemy can't see through the fire, so drop TNT blocks behind it. Pull away from the firewall, shooting through it at the enemy. If hit, the enemy will usually kite, following you through the firewall. This will light them on fire, running them into the TNT and blowing them up. Works even better if you can put it in a pit and then escape out of the top of it. NOTE: Most items and blocks are destroyed by TNT. You will probably still find some resources that were hit with the shock-wave, however.

The Sato Technique. Set a TNT trap by digging down two blocks and placing one TNT block at the bottom of the pit. Put a block that can take a Pressure Plate above the TNT and put a Pressure Plate on it. Now kite a mob or enemy over the plate, and if you can keep them in the general vicinity, they'll go sky-high when the TNT detonates. Also works best in a pit. NOTE: Also destroys most items. But is really, really funny. Can also be used as a trap around your base, but not too close of course (unless you've got an Obsidian blast wall).

Advanced Redstone & Inventions

If getting to 'The End' is the culmination of the adventure part of Minecraft, being able to incorporate Redstone into your builds is the pinnacle of construction. This is easier said than done, as Redstone and its mechanisms are basically a fully functioning system of electric power and circuitry, and a truly complete knowledge of the feature is almost impossible (even the guys who build computers out of it always have something else to learn).

Despite that, graduating from basic Lever-and-Door setups isn't all that hard, and learning the basic building blocks of various systems that can be combined into more complex builds shouldn't be hard for most player who give it a go.

In order to get your wheels turning and start the path to your Redstone mastery, here are some projects to try out in your worlds. We'll start with the simple fun of a few traps before we move on to some of the basic circuit types.

Traps

A good trap setup correctly and activated at the right time is one of the best things in Minecraft. Seeing a Creeper unsuspectingly step on a rigged plate before exploding, or tricking another player into falling to their doom is thoroughly rewarding, and they're experiences you're likely to have when you build one of these bad boys.

Death Wall

You don't have to leave your house to murder mobs. The Death Wall turns your house into a death-dispensing fortress controlled by just a Lever and a little Redstone, and it's not too hard to set up.

This trap takes advantage of the fact that a Dispenser filled with an Arrow stack will fire its Arrows when powered. While you can always just leave some full Dispensers lying about your map with a Pressure Plate in front of them (so they attack the mob that steps on them), you're unlikely to do a whole lot of damage this way. Instead, incorporate the concept into your home by placing Dispensers in your walls facing outward. Put a stack or two of Arrows in these and connect all Dispensers to one Lever in your house with Redstone.

If you get it wired up right, the Dispensers will fire a volley of Arrows at whatever is in front of them when you flip the Lever. Flip it off and then on again, and they'll fire again, and you can repeat the action until the Arrows run out. This is actually faster than Buttons, and is quite devastating.

This is easiest when the back of the Dispensers are exposed on the inside wall of your house, but if you play around with burying your Redstone lines, you can create some highly destructive firing patterns with Dispensers shooting across the land outside your base from various angles. This method is also one of the better PVP defense mechanisms, though players can always steal arrows from your Dispensers.

Simple TNT traps are fun and also quite funny, though only beginner players will be fooled by them.

Miner's First TNT Trap

TNT traps are without question the most popular way for miners to get a trick kill on other miners, and though they're not great when it comes to keeping dropped loot intact, they are some of the most entertaining things to build in the game. On top of, and perhaps because of that, players have gotten ridiculously creative over the years with various styles of TNT traps, but almost everybody starts with one basic trap.

That is the Pressure Plate TNT trap, the most basic explosive trap in the game. All it takes is digging a hole two blocks deep, then putting a TNT block at the bottom. Put a block of another material on top of the TNT block, and then put a Pressure Plate on that. When players run over, a few seconds later the area will blow up.

Now, you'll probably catch a few players here and there with this simple version of the trap, but because it takes a few seconds and players usually run away, not to mention that it's pretty easy to see the Pressure Plate, this trap is too basic to kill most players or mobs. Luckily, it's one of the easiest to tweak with more TNT, more Redstone, or disguises for the trap, so just play around with it!

Note how the Torches keep the Sand from falling. Using this method, you can create a Sand floor of any shape that can be taken out by just one piston.

Fake Floor of Hilarity

If you place a Torch on a block, you can then place another block on the space above the first block, and then place a block of Sand or Gravel on the space above the Torch. Since this block of Sand or Gravel doesn't have an actual block below it (just a Torch), it would usually fall, but the Torch keeps it up. By combining this feature with the fact that a layer of Sand will fall if the layer supporting it falls, we can create one of the most dramatic and funny traps in the game, the Fake Floor of Hilarity.

You'll want to check out the photos for this one, because it's a little different than the kinds of builds many players are used to. Essentially what happens is that a player walks over a Pressure Plate to open an Iron Door to a room (a Chest on the far wall can help to entice players). As they walk into the room, the Iron Door slams shut behind them, and they get stuck as there is no way to open the Door from the inside. Before they can decide to break out, the Sand floor beneath their feet suddenly starts collapsing until the entire floor has fallen out of the room and down a huge pit, taking the player with them.

Here's a basic breakdown of what you need to do to create this tricky fake room: first dig a big pit that's either far enough down to kill or do big damage to the tricked player (or that has something damaging at the bottom like Cactus, fire etc.). In the middle of the pit, build a one-block tower of Sand up out of the pit to at least 6 blocks below ground level. Now put Torches on each side of the top block on the tower. Make the tower one block of Sand taller, and then put blocks of Sand on all sides of that block. Because the Torches are below, they will stay in place despite having no block beneath them. You can then put Torches on the sides of the new layer of Sand blocks and repeat with a third layer.

Screenshot: Minecraft® ™ & © 2009–2013 Mojang/Notch.

You'll have to bury the Redstone, of course, but this exposed view shows how the Pressure Plate is wired to both the Iron Door and the Redstone below, which leads to the Piston.

By repeating this process and placing Torches and blocks in the right place, you can eventually create a flat rectangle of Sand that can be used as a floor (or another shape, if you want). Then, build a room of some sturdy, regular building material around the Sand floor, adding an Iron Door as the only entrance.

If you calculate this right so that the floor of Sand is about level with the ground outside, and if you put it in an area where a Sand floor doesn't seem weird, you're very likely to trick other players into thinking that they've come across a normal room. Adding items like a Chest across from the Door in a little alcove in the wall, or maybe some items set on the Sand or walls, will also help draw in the unsuspecting.

But before you can trap your friends with your sweet, sweet fake house, you need to wire it up with Redstone. This is pretty simple: start with

a Pressure Plate in front of the Iron Door and then put a Piston up against one of the blocks on the one block tower that holds up your fake floor. Wire the Piston to the Pressure Plate (make sure this is hidden) so that stepping on the Plate opens the Door and also makes the Piston shove one of the blocks out of the supporting one-block-wide tower.

Because of the way Sand (and Gravel) acts, the first block falling out of the supporting tower causes the block of Sand above it to fall as well, which causes anything supported by it to fall as well. The resulting chain reaction means each level above the block that the Piston shoved will fall one by one, eventually causing the entire floor to collapse into the pit below it. At this point anyone who has entered your house is either dead, or at the least very hurt and stuck in a pit with nothing to show for it.

The House Cleaner in cut-away. See how it starts with a small amount of Water that is spread by the Stone below.

This is the kind of pattern that you should use to spread the stream of Water.

The House Cleaner

One of the neater projects we've ever seen in person was a system that used Water and Redstone to clean out an entire house whenever a Lever was pulled, and this really isn't too hard to set up in smaller homes or those that plan it out from the get-go. When it comes to counteracting home invasions, whether of the mob or other player sort, The House Cleaner is among the best, as it's quick, doesn't mess up most of your stuff and can be turned off easily.

To build, start pretty high above the rooms you want your system to flood. Build a trench three blocks long and two blocks deep, then remove one of the blocks at the bottom of one end of the trench. Two blocks away from this, place a Sticky Piston so that it's facing where the block was, and then attach a block to it. Wire this Piston up with Redstone to a Lever in a spot in your house that will be safe from the Water, so that when you flip the Lever the Piston pushes the block it is attached to back into the bottom of the trench, closing the hole.

At the top of the other end of the Trench, drop a Water Bucket so that the Water flows through the trench and down out the hole when the Piston is pulled back. When you flip the Lever so the Piston moves forward again, it should then close the hole in the trench, blocking the flow of Water.

Under the hole in the trench, leave a few blocks, and then place five blocks in the shape of a cross (one in the center with a block on all sides). Four or five blocks below this, build a rectangular structure of blocks with holes in it every other block (a kind of honeycomb shape, see picture). When you pull the Lever and the hole opens in the trench, the Water will flow out of the hole and hit the blocks built below it, splitting the flow into multiple flows and widening it so that it can clean out entire rooms.

Building this for one room is easy (just make the flow as wide as the room), allowing you to turn the switch on and off so that the Water flows through and then drains out very quickly. Building it for a complex structure or your whole base will take a lot more work and will involve a great deal of planning, but it can be done, and it ends up being a very useful and fun addition to your build.

Most of the primary types of Redstone Gates.

Useful Redstone Circuitry

The preceding builds are all a lot of fun and take a bit of Redstone know-how, but neither the builds in this version of Minecrafter nor those in the last even come close to encompassing all that can be done with this powerful game feature. Learning all of the things Redstone can do is really not that different at all from learning how real electronic currents, wiring and even programming work, and some Redstone builds are so complex that you literally need a degree to understand what's going on.

That being said, there are some fairly simple Redstone structures (called "circuits") that are essentially the building blocks for more complex Redstone builds, and by learning them and using them together, you'll be be able to amplify the quality and scope of your Redstone achievements many times over.

NOTE: Interestingly, these "circuits" work almost exactly the same in real life wiring and computing as they do with Redstone, and they've all been around for a very long time.

NOT Gate

The NOT Gate is the simplest advanced Redstone circuit, and it has a very useful function: it reverses the effect of a powered line. So say you have a Piston attached to a Lever: add a NOT Gate between the Piston and the Lever, and instead of making the Piston extend when the Lever is flipped and the Redstone line is powered, it makes the Piston pull back. This is incredibly useful when used on Redstone wires that branch, as you can make one Lever, Button or other such feature do different things to different mechanisms (like make one door open and another close).

To build the NOT Gate, put a Lever down and then a Redstone wire going out from it one block. After the wire, place a block down on the same line as the Lever and the wire are on. On the opposite side of the block to the Lever, place a Redstone Torch. On the block past the Torch (still on line with the Lever for this first one, though you can change it in later builds when you've got the hang of it), place another Redstone wire and then connect this to whatever mechanism you want. When you flip the lever, it will power the wire, which will turn off the Redstone Torch, leaving the mechanism without power. Flip it again, Torch comes back on, mechanism functions.

AND Gate

The second type of gate, and perhaps the one you'll hear about most often when players are talking about complex builds, is the AND Gate. Where the NOT gate reverses the power of a Redstone wire, the AND Gate is used to tell a mechanism that it can't function unless two power sources are functioning on it. This means if the AND Gate is attached to two Levers, both must be turned on for the signal to send to the mechanism beyond.

To build, start with two Levers set down going the same direction with Redstone wires coming off of each, also going the same direction (so there should be one block of space between the wires. At the end of each wire, place a block and then place a block between those two. There should now be a line of three blocks , two Redstone wires coming out of the two end blocks, and two

Levers on the other side of the wires. On top of the blocks you just placed, put a Redstone Torch at either and and then a Redstone wire between the Torches. On the other side of the blocks from the Levers, pace a Redstone Torch on the side of the middle block. On the block on the ground in front of that third Redstone Torch, place another wire down, and then a mechanism after that.

When a switch is thrown, it sends a current through the wire in front of it to one of the Redstone Torches on top of the blocks and turns it off. If both of these are turned off, the Redstone wire between the two Redstone Torches on top of the block goes underpowered, which turns on the Redstone Torch on the side of the blocks. This then powers the line on the other side of the blocks from the Levers. Turn either Lever off, and the signal does not get through.

Other Gates

There are many types of Redstone circuits and gates out there, with some of the most prominent being the NAND (NOT Gate + AND Gate), the OR Gate (functions if either power source is on, but not if both are), the NOR Gate, the XOR Gate and the NXOR, and all of them are incredibly useful for advance builds. In fact, knowing when and how to use these gates is what really sets the master players apart, and they fittingly can take a very long time to become good at.

Repeating Signal

Rails, especially Powered Rails and Detector Rails, are also very important when it comes to building advanced Redstone circuits. This is because of the fact that Minecarts take time to travel over Rails, but they can also run over Detector Rails and thus send a signal, so you can use Rails and Minecarts to cause signals to happen at certain times.

There are many, many Rail and Minecart circuits out there, some of which get seriously complex, but here's a fun and easy one to get you started. It's a very quick system that, when built and started up, sends a steady pulsing signal through a Redstone circuit forever until part of the system is destroyed.

Setup requires that you dig an area down that is seven blocks long, one block deep and at least two blocks wide. Lay down a straight line of Rail in this pattern: Powered Rail-Detector Rail-Regular Rail-Detector Rail-Regular Rail-Detector

Rail-Power Rail. Lead a Redstone wire from the Detector Rail in the center of the track to whatever mechanism you want to power, as this is where the signal will come from. Attach a second Redstone wire to one of the Powered Rails, and attach that to a Lever or Button. Place a Minecart on that end of the track, and when you flip the Lever, it will send the Minecart going along the track, hitting the Detector Rails in the process.

Because there is a Detector and Power Rail at each end of the track, the Minecart will keep bouncing from one end of the track to the other forever, hitting the Detector in the middle every time and sending a signal from it in a pulsing pattern.

This is very, very useful for automated processes and for complex Redstone circuits in advanced builds, and if you start messing with Redstone quite a bit, it's likely you'll find a use for it in no time flat.

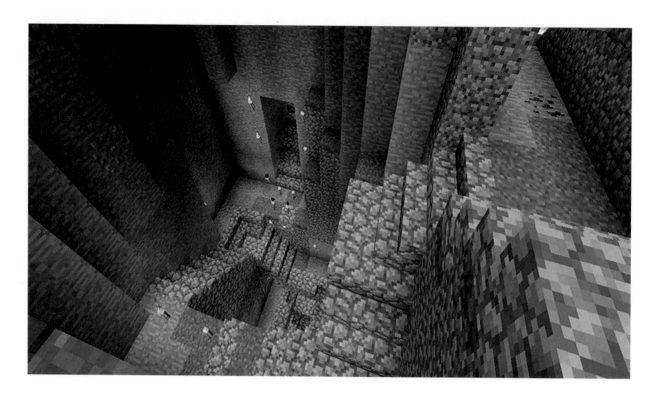

Mine Better

When it's time to slam a Pickaxe into some Stone, you need to be ready to go. There's gonna be a lot going on out there in your mine, from caves to explore, to mobs that'll attack you, to ore to snag and more, and it's easy to get distracted (and killed). Remember miner: when you put Pickaxe into hand and you set out for ore, you've got one goal, and that's to mine as well as you darn can.

To do that, you need to do three things: find resources, extract them, and return them to be stored in a safe area in as large amounts as is possible and as fast as is possible without dying.

To do that more often than you end up dead and far from your base, you need to keep a few things in mind.

The Camp

Perhaps the best habit you can adopt for yourself as a miner is to never mine far from a base. This doesn't mean you need to stay by your home, far from it. We just mean that if you're mining and there isn't a Chest or five, a Crafting Table, a Furnace, maybe a Bed and certainly some safe, safe walls to get to quickly, you're mining dangerously.

Mining free, with a base farther than a minute or so away, is a fine tactic when you're out exploring, just starting a world or otherwise unable to invest any large amount of time into the effort, but once you've established a home, you should rarely be mining without having a secure area nearby in which to resupply, deposit gathered resources and hide from the elements.

Camps can be built just about anywhere, as all you need to do is build a small room wherever you are. Don't hesitate to wall off a section of a cave or build a safehouse within a structure like a ravine, Fortress or any other. You have mastery over this land, if you'll take it, and you can never really have enough safehouses.

To produce the best results, plan your mines by first picking a good spot for a mining camp/safehouse, such as at the bottom of a deep staircase, or built up in a natural structure such as a ravine or cave. Bring the stuff you'll need to build a good camp along with you to the spot you want to mine before actually mining, and it will make your ore collection progress much quicker than it otherwise would.

Well-lit tunnels are a must for any good camp.

Another shot of a good mining camp, complete with Chests, a Crafting Table and a furnace.

Camps can be as elaborate or simple as you'd like, but each should meet a few requirements: they should be secure from mobs (meaning they should be well-lit and only accessible through Doors or Trapdoors), they should be easily accessible from your mine (no more than a minute or two away from where you're mining), and they should contain a Chest with helpful items, a Crafting Table, a Furnace and possibly a Bed at the least.

Good items to bring to start a base include Wood of any kind (as well as Planks and Sticks), Cobblestone, tools and weapons, food, and Coal, Charcoal and Torches. Unless you expand your mining camps into more permanent bases, you should think of them as places to resupply and work temporarily, so transport rare or valuable items back to your main bases when you can.

This Miner has all the gear he needs to set out in search of ore.

Don't forget the armor and the Sword when you go minin'!

For Mining

3 or 4 Stone Pickaxes

2 or 3 Stone Shovels

At least 2 Pickaxes of higher quality

At least 1 Shovel of higher quality

1 full stack of Torches or more
(4 stacks is a good number)

Enough food to get full from empty three times
(cooked meat and Bread are great options)

1 full stack of Cobblestone, 2 at most (partially
in order to make a Furnace)

Whatever Wood you can spare (a full stack of
Wood is ideal, but at least some Wood, Wood
Planks and/or Wood Sticks is a very good idea)

When First Setting Up Base Add

As many Torches as you can

As much Coal as you can

As much Wood as you can

3 more Shovels and Pickaxes of any type
except Wood or Gold

2 or more Chests

1 Crafting Table

Some Iron Ore or Iron Ingots

The Gear

A Pickaxe is all you need to mine, but it's not the only item you should take with you on your trips. When you need to mine, plan an extensive mining excursion that takes a bit of time and gear, and your trips will be much more rewarding.

Miners out on a serious resource acquiring jaunt should take as much of the following kit as possible for best results. You might not be able to acquire all of this gear at first, so just take as much as you can and improve your kit as you expand. Eventually, you'll be able to add to this kit and outdo it by adding better items as you progress in your world.

Each time you go out on a planned trip to mine, take the mining kit with you, and stay out mining until you use it all up or run out of inventory space. By doing this and combining it with the practices below, you'll end up with the maximum number of resources in the least amount of time.

The Exploratory Trips

As tempting as it might be, don't go just randomly mining when you find a cave or other structure (or at least don't do so for long). Plan your trips, get your gear ready, know where your base is, and head out with an area in mind.

• The best mines are centered around a mineshaft (a vertical shaft with a ladder) or a staircase that goes from ground level to the bedrock. Build tunnels or clear out levels around these, never going too far from the center staircase or mineshaft and always going straight out from the center. No twisting passages or changing levels, just straight halls, rooms and tunnels with flat floors.

• Keep your mine organized, but also collect all resources you see. When you find ore, follow it and mine it all out, but when it's done, repair your mine so that you keep it easy to understand. For instance, if you come across some ore that goes below the level that the rest of your mine is on, mine it out and then replace the floor so that it stays flat.

• Remember the two rules of ore finding: ore is most common below level 16 and near Lava. If you're really looking for ore, you want to have a base in the lower levels so you can explore them, and you want to look out for Lava. When you find Lava, dig around it, containing it as you go, and you'll more than likely come across some nice resource deposits.

Best Mining Practices

Some general tips for mining, these will refine your tactics into well-developed, highly efficient processes.

- Use tools to breaking. You're already out, and though you might have some other project you feel like rushing off to, you're best served by using up the tools you have when you're already in your mine. If you take our mining kit with you and use it all up, you'll collect more resources each time you're out, making the time you spent in your mine much more worthwhile.

- Your mine should have a straight shot to the surface. We've covered this a bit before, but it bears reiteration, as it's so key to good mining. It should never be hard to get back to the surface from your mine, and if it is, you should make an easy exit for yourself.

- You should have a quick shot back to base when mining as well. Again, we've covered this but we're going to say it again: it should never take more than a minute or two to get back to a base from where you're mining. Keep mining far away from base and we can tell you from experience that a Creeper's gonna find you and ruin your day sooner than later.

- Deposit resources often. It's a guaranteed win when you take your resources back to your secure base no matter how little or how much you've gathered. Do it as much as possible.

- Leave no dark spots in your mines. No matter how small the shadowy spots are in your mine, light them up. You should never, ever have mobs spawning in the areas you are mining, and you can make that happen by using Torches and other light sources liberally.

- Use signs to direct yourself. Whether it's telling you what level you're on or that a cave or base is "This Way," use signs. There's never going to be a moment where you are sad that a sign told you where something is, and there will be many times you wish there was one to help out.

- Keep your tools close together in your tray. Switching between tools like Pickaxes and Shovels can take up a lot of time over many switches, so keep them right next to each other and you'll save a lot of minutes.

- Go in pairs, with one player mining and the other organizing. If playing multiplayer, split the responsibilities by having one player expand the mine and gather resources while the other cleans up behind them and keeps the mine organized. It really is worth the trouble.

- Leave a third of your Iron tools by switching to Stone for mining lesser materials. Use your Iron tools on all materials until there's about a third of them left. Then switch to Stone tools unless you find something that requires Iron to break. This allows you to stay out longer, as you can still collect the more valuable ores while continuing to expand your mine.

The Bedrock Tunnel

This mining strategy technically belongs in the structures section, but as its purpose is almost exclusively related to mining, we've included it here.

In our mining (and even exploring) of the Minecraft world, few structures have come in as handy as The Bedrock Tunnel, which is exactly what it sounds like. By digging down to the Bedrock and building a well-organized cavern or tunnel, you are able to expand over large areas of the map easily, giving you access to the layers above. The terrain right above teh Bedrock level is almost always solid Stone and ore, with maybe a little Lava and Gravel, so you can usually count on being able to dig out a simple rectangular room or tunnel with ease.

This tunnel or room can then be expanded on (we've even seem some Crafters who dug out the entire bottom layer of the map, incredibly), and you can build mineshafts with Ladders up out of the Bedrock Tunnel to access the entire map above. This means that you can use your Bedrock Tunnel to test out various areas of the map for caves, ravines, Fortresses and other structures while having an easy area to return to (the Bedrock Tunnel) that contains safe-houses and eventually leads back to your main base. Add rails and Minecarts for even quicker access to the entire map.

Advanced Farming

Runnin' around and a'murderin' mobs in order to get food, or making maniacal runs on Villager Wheat farms, is all well and good, and will get you through the beginning of the game just fine. However, later in the game, having to leave your base for food trips can get exceedingly tedious and frustrating, and it usually leads to a cycle of taking quick hunting trips that never gather enough food, leading you have to go huntin' again not too far in the future.

In the end, having a ready food source built into your home such as a farm or ranch is almost a must for a Minecrafter, and they really aren't too hard to set up. Last Minecrafter we showed you a few neat and efficient ways to build some basic, high-yield farms and ranches that you can use to keep your food close and easy to get to, but despite making it a lot easier to acquire food than it would be by hunting, our farms and ranches still required you to do a bit of work when it comes to harvesting the food.

This being Minecraft, however, there is almost always a way to turn most tasks into automated systems that require very little input, and this is certainly the case with farms. If you want to step up your food acquisition game to the next level, give these builds a go.

Two Styles of Automated Farms

Piston Farms can easily be attached to most existing farms.

The Piston Farmer

Pistons are one of the most dynamic and useful objects in the Minecraft universe, and when it comes to farming, they can help you out quite a lot. This build takes advantage of the fact that an activated Piston that shoves over a plot of grown Wheat will cause the Wheat to break and drop so you can grab it and use it.

This build can be added to most farms, but you'll need to leave at least one or two blocks next to each block where you will grow Wheat. All you need to do then is place a Piston on the empty block one block next to and one block above the block on which you're growing the Wheat. Make sure the Piston faces the Wheat, and do this for every block where there will be Wheat. Then, wire all of the Pistons together with Redstone so that they lead to one single Lever. (You may need some Repeaters.)

Screenshot: Minecraft® ™ & © 2009–2013 Mojang/Notch.

The Water Scythe caught in action as it harvests Wheat for you.

When you flip the Lever, all Pistons should extend across where the Wheat has grown, breaking the Wheat. Flip the Lever again so that the Pistons detract, and where there once was a Wheat farm, there is now a large amount of Wheat icons floating on empty patches of Dirt, and you can just run down your farm and grab them, replanting as you go.

The Water Scythe

Piston farming's fun, but when it comes to efficiency, nothing beats the Water Scythe. Like Pistons, Water that flows over a block of growing Wheat will break it. Unlike Pistons, however, flowing Water will actually carry the dropped Wheat with it.

By using both of these features, we can harvest an entire farm with the flick of a Lever and direct the flow of the Water so that all of the harvested Wheat gathers in one spot for you to pick up.

For this, you'll want to build your farm in a terrace formation, with one level of the farm one block below the other. Before you plant, go to the far end of the top level of your farm, and build a little wall with alcoves (holes) in it that line up with where the Wheat will be planted. Now, place Buckets of Water in the alcoves so that it flows out over the whole farmland, making sure that it doesn't overflow the sides. Test this out a bit so that you get it right.

Now move to the bottom level of your farm and see where the water is flowing out. Build around this so that all of the Water collects in one trench that goes downhill and ends in one single block (without overflowing).

Go back to the top of your farm and temporarily remove the Water. What you need to do now is control when the Water comes out. The best way to do this is by building a system of Sticky Pistons, blocks and a Lever, so that when you push the Lever, the Pistons remove the blocks from in front of the Water, allowing it to flow (and when you push it again, the Pistons put the blocks back and stop the Water). If you don't have or don't want to use Sticky Pistons, however, you can simply use a block of Dirt over the alcove that you punch out when you want to harvest your Wheat.

Once it's all set up, plant your Wheat and wait until harvest day, which will be the easiest one you've ever had.

Semi-Automated Breeding

An above view of the somewhat-workable Automated Breeding machine.

Unfortunately, the console version of the game is not yet set up to where we can have fully automated breeding, as there's no way to automate feeding animals Wheat yet, but you can set up a fun if not always well-functioning automated breeder using a few Powered Rails, Detector Rails and some Water.

Start your build with a pen for your selected animal. Make the pen lead to two Fence Gates that are separated by one block and that have a drop off immediately after them. You want your pen to funnel animals toward the Gates one at a time, and it's best if you can isolate two animals (one in front of each gate) if possible, so play around with Fences, Fence Gates, trenches and other methods to find the one that works best for you.

On the other side of each Gate (one block down from them), build a railway in this pattern: Powered Rail-Detector Rail-3 to 5 regular Rails-Detector Rail-Powered Rail. Make sure that there is a block at the end of the railway to stop the Minecart as well.

The machine in action!

In the space between the two rails, dig a trench that starts one block deep and then one block before the end of the rails goes two blocks deep, and then three deep one block beyond that. Build a little pool at the end, and then dump a Bucket of Water at the top of the trench by the Gates so that it flows away from the pen and past the railways into the pool. Build a Fence immediately around your rails, blocking off the end so that animals can go under the Fence and into the pool, but never outside of the build.

Bone Meal

Note that these Pigs were brought down the canal and into the pen below, making them easy to harvest Pork from.

Finally, fill your pen with animals and set two Minecarts, one on each railway right in front of the fence. Use Wheat to put two animals into love mode (with the hearts above) and then open the Gates and lure them onto the carts.

What should happen if all goes well is that the animals in love will fall into the Minecarts, which will bounce down the track and then back again forever. As they pass each other, you should start to see baby animals pop up between them, which will hopefully fall into the Water and be pushed out into the pool.

Works for Chickens...and Cows too, as well as other breed-able mobs (though it still can get messed up just as easily).

What can often happen, however, is that you will find it hard to get the mobs both in love mode and into the carts, and the baby mobs can often get in the way of the tracks meaning you need to give the carts a little push. You also tend to have to put animals back into love mode once they fall out, which can be hard to do while on carts.

It's not the best system, but it's pretty easy and fun to build, and as of right now, it's the best we've got for automated breeding. Tweak it here and there, such as maybe making there be a drop under the rails to where the water flows (so baby mobs simply have nowhere else to spawn), and you may be able to achieve better results. Hopefully in future they'll make this a little easier!

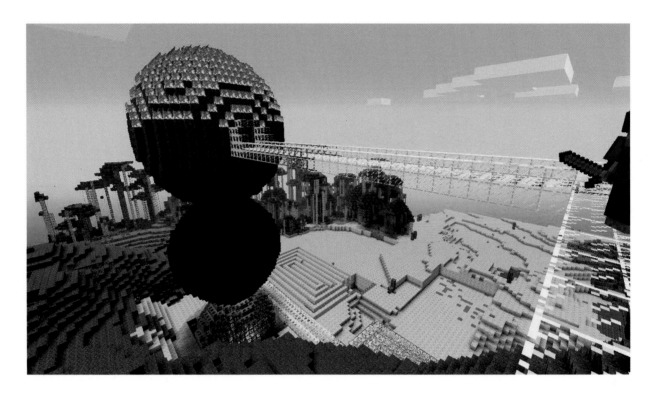

Building Advanced Structures

Now that you've been crafting a bit, you're probably ready to move beyond the basic house and want to sink your teeth into some serious builds. While the magic of Minecraft is that every person will find different ways to build their creations, we can help you in your quest to take your structures to the next level with these tips and ideas. Add your own touch to these, or use them in your own builds, and you'll find your world will soon be covered in unique architectural masterpieces.

Tips for Structure Pieces

Before we get to the big builds, here are some tips on incorporating commonly-used features into your structures. Most every build can be improved by a good staircase or window, and there's more to think about than just punching holes in walls for light or throwing down a stair or two.

Staircase

It's really, really easy to build a structure and then try and fit a staircase in it and fail miserably at making it look good and well-organized. This is because staircases need a certain amount of space, and we often build the main structure without making sure it has the necessary room for a staircase.

Remember this when making a staircase: the smallest workable staircase goes up at least two blocks and out at least three while being at least two blocks wide. This staircase is the bare minimum, and you have to remove the blocks you use to build the actual stair pieces on after you place them in order to have enough room to use the staircase.

Keep this in mind as you're building, and test your area as you go using blocks of Dirt in place of where your stairs will be. If you use Dirt blocks to see how and if a staircase will fit in your new build when you've only built one or two levels of it, you'll be able to make any adjustments to the floor plan before you build much. This can save a lot of time and effort, as it's often the case that a large section of a building has to be removed and tweaked in order to fit in a good staircase.

Another method is to build your staircases attached to the main building in their own little tower that's outside the rest (think parking garage staircases). This doesn't always fit with a build, but it can give you lots of room inside the main structure and add an aesthetic flair to your build if done well.

One final thought is to build the staircase around the entire outside of your building. This looks very cool on towers and is best for structures that are taller than they are wide, but it can also be a little dangerous if you don't add some Fences as railing.

Screenshot: Minecraft® ™ & © 2009–2013 Mojang/Notch.

Villager houses show an easy way to make a flat-ended pyramid roof with stairs.

Another pyramid-style design for a roof.

Roofs

Roofs are, for the most part, pretty easy to make, but we have just three thingswe wanted to mention that we think will improve your roof-building game.

Don't feel confined to flat roofs. Most builders start off their first few structures as just square buildings with flat roofs, and these are fine, but try out a pyramid-style roof. They're very easy and have an attractive look about them, and they separate your houses from those of a newby.

Use Stairs to give roofs a different texture. Stairs are kind-of the unofficial shingles of the Minecraft world, and using them on your roof will break up the monotony of blocky roofs.

Consider giving the roof a lip. Whether flat, terraced or otherwise built (we've seen some

Use different colored blocks in patterns on roofs for neat symmetrical effects.

awesome domes, which we'll talk about below!), think about giving the edge of your roof a lip, meaning it sticks out at least a block over the wall of the structure below. Besides looking good, this actually has a very practical reason: it keeps Spiders from being able to climb to the top of your home. Spiders can only go up straight walls or inclines, but can't make it over a lip. If you keep finding those pesky pixelated arachnids on top of your house, you might want to give this a go.

Domes are just awesome-looking, and can also provide protection from mobs while allowing sunlight in!

Windows

These windows are low, so using Glass is the best idea.

Of all these structures, windows are the ones where you're probably going, "Hey, I can build a window, man." Well, that's probably true, we can all punch a hole in a wall and let the light in, but can you build a good window? Here are some tips to help you, some of which are common sense and some that you might not have thought of yet.

Never just leave an empty space as a window unless you're very high up. This is something that we all do, but shouldn't, and those who continue to do so will find out why eventually when a Skeleton shoots through, a Creeper blows up or a Spider sneaks in. Always cover up your window with something at lower levels, unless you're absolutely sure nothing will be able to see in and try and attack you. Annoying darn Skeletons.

Use Glass or Glass panes at lower levels, never Fences, except for one-block wide murder holes. Place murder holes (one-block windows with a fence in them) in areas where there's plenty of room to move around, and use them by peeking out and shooting arrows through at the mobs beyond, then ducking away if needed (such as when fighting those pesky Skeletons).

A solid row of Fence windows going all the way around a building will keep Spiders from climbing up to your roof. Spiders can't crawl over Fences (nothin' can!), so using them at the top of a build all the way around it will effectively remove the Spider threat from your roof.

Windows don't have to only go in buildings!

Build little pool areas for the Elevator to deposit into (to avoid spills)

Water Elevator

They're not exactly the most realistic architectural feature you're going to have in your house, but when you need to go up and down a long way quickly and without having to spend a lot of resources or time building a Ladder or Stairs, you want a Water Elevator. Building one is about as easy as it gets: find a place where you want to be able to go from high to low (or vice versa) quickly, and drop a Bucket of Water so that it flows over the side of your high spot and down below. You'll want to build a little pool for the Water to catch in, and placing the Bucket of Water in a little controlled cubby at the top of the elevator can help keep it contained to one block (you usually only want them one block wide, bigger gets complicated).

This hole of Water looks unassuming, but it's actually an elevator that goes all the way to the Bedrock.

These tried-and-true, well-used structures are awesome for getting to and from deep mines or high castles, though you do need to make sure that the elevator is not too long, as you will have to breathe at some point. Most Crafters have at least one or two of these around their map, and you just have to try one out to see how useful they are.

Note: Some Crafters make small one or two block wide pools on the surface that look like plain water ponds, but when you dive in, they actually take you down to a secret base! Of course, if someone falls in or sees you dive in and not come back out, you might have an uninvited guest sooner rather than later.

Some Crafters have experimented with different shapes and styles to create fancier Elevators, some of which utilize Boats.

Screenshot: Minecraft® ™ & © 2009–2013 Mojang/Notch.

Structures

And now for the real meat: the big structure ideas. Use these as a jumping-off point for your own builds, or try one out when you're bored and looking for a new project. More than likely, you'll find something to add or make your own with these, and that's what Minecraft is all about, young Crafter.

Start your tower by shaping it out on the ground with Dirt first.

Towers Done Right

Nothing says "accomplished Crafter with awesome buildin' skills" like a big darn tower shooting up off of a mountain-top, and they're often one of the first advanced structures that Crafters build after their initial house.

The primary thing to keep in mind when building a tower is that you should plan out the build a bit before you get going. Take a look at our tips on staircases above, and make sure before you build too much that you know how you are going to incorporate a way to get up and down your new tower. Staircase? Ladder? Water elevator? They all work, but they all require a little planning to do well.

Also, think about whether you want the tower to just look cool or whether it should have room to do things in. You have to build your tower's base pretty large to accommodate both a staircase and rooms to do things in, so keep that in mind when planning. One good trick is to make most of the bottom part of the tower the housing for a grand staircase which goes up to a single floor and ends. Build more floors above that floor, but use a series of Ladders to get between these top floors instead of a staircase. This allows you to have a neat staircase (always prettier than just a Ladder), a tall tower and some rooms to put things in.

Another idea to consider is to make your entire tower a useful, functioning piece of your world by making it into a lighthouse. Adding a bunch of Torches or Glowstone to your tower at the top will allow it to be seen from quite far away (if there's nothing tall in the way, like a mountain or Jungle Biome), which is very helpful when navigating the wild. Not only does it tell you where home is, it gives you a constant focus point, which does wonders for learning the land around your base.

The inside of a completed tower.

The Great Pit

When it comes to easy-to-navigate mining structures that allow for excellent ore-finding and also look really cool, the Giant Pit is one of the best. Essentially just a big hole all the way down to the Bedrock, these work great when you start one a few levels beneath your base and, and they can add a dramatic flair to your home (while also providing a huge number of resources).

Construction of these is deceptively simple: all you need to do is dig down in a predetermined shape (usually just a square). However, if you've never undertaken removing this much material from one area, it can take a lot longer than you'd expect. The best method we've found is to cut out the border of the shape you'd want, and then walk along it row by row pointing down and mining out as many blocks as you can reach. Stand on the row behind the one you're mining, and then move back one row after you mine the whole row in front of you out.

At some point in your Pit, build a little base so that you don't have to go all the way up to your main base constantly.

For greatest efficiency, leave any ore you uncover that's outside of your shape alone for now and go back to them later, using them as reference points to start horizontal mineshafts off of your pit. You should also build a staircase along the edge of your pit as you work and add a one-block thick column up the center that goes back to your base by means of a Ladder. Use the staircases to move around the outside and work on various levels, while the Ladder in the center is for easy entrance and exit from the pit. Of course, this project is going to move along much quicker if mining together with a friend.

Like towers, Pits work best when drawn out beforehand.

Once done, put a little base at the bottom of the pit, and you'll have quick access to every level, not to mention having uncovered quite a bit of ore and possibly even some structures.

Note: If you crack into a ravine, Fortress or other structure, continue the shape of your pit by walling it off from the structure you've cracked into. Mark where the structure is, or better yet use Glass as the walls, and you'll be able to access it easily and much more safely than you normally would (another bonus of the Great Pit).

A completed Water base from the outside.

The Underwater Base

Who doesn't want to live underwater, right? In Minecraft this is totally possible, but it does take some planning. If you swim down and try to just build some walls and put a roof on it, you're going to notice that your house is sort-of totally filled up with Water, which isn't exactly easy to live in. Plus it lets Squids in your home, which is just weird.

In order to build a base that won't drown you, you need to build the shape of the structure you want and then mine out the middle of it. Do this by making the shape of the building you want with blocks (fill the whole thing in as you go, don't leave any part hollow). Once you've got the shape of the building completed, put a Door down right in front of where you want the actual Door to be (so one block in front of your structure on the ocean floor). Doors are one of a few items that when placed cause Water to repel away from them, so you can then open the Door and punch out the two blocks behind it (in the shape of the Door) without flooding the space they leave with Water.

Once you've started into your base, hollow out the rest of it, making sure to plug up any holes you create quickly before the Water can flow in and fill the base. Once you've got it hollowed out, you can start adding things to it like you normally would to a base, and you can even make windows if you're quick enough to drop a block in quickly.

The primary problem, of course, with building underwater bases is staying underwater long enough to build without drowning. In order to do this, use the trick where Water will not flow through certain blocks that you can then move to. Ladders, Doors and Fences all leave at least some space around them that you can stick your head into and breathe, but Water does not enter the blocks they are on, meaning you can build little underwater breathing areas with these items.

Crafter Darkscour took the underwater base to a whole 'nother level with this one.

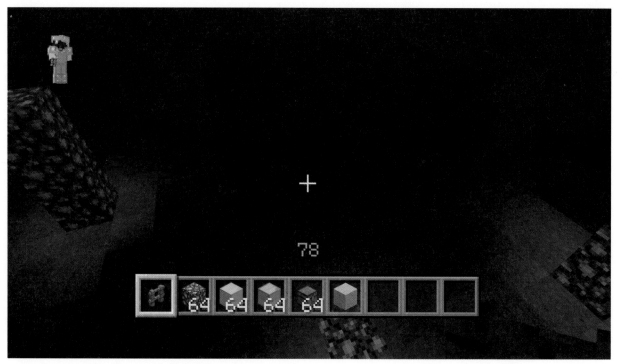

Dropping a shell like this one from above helps you avoid having to be underwater without air for as long.

Use an outline like this one to make it easier to drop your Sand or Gravel.

Another method is to use gravity-influenced blocks like Sand or Gravel to build the shape of your structure from above, dropping them down so they fall through the Water and down to where you want them. You'll still have to swim down and put down a door, and you'll need to replace the outer layer with something solid like Stone (or surround the whole thing and just mine out the Sand), but this method can make your planning go much quicker overall.

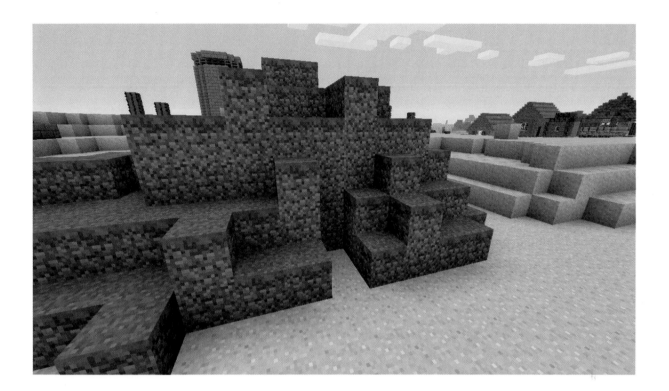

The Double Bluff Base

Getting robbed or having your home damaged by other players online is less common on the console than on the PC version, but attacks like this (called "griefing") do happen. It has become common practice in PVP (or just busy) servers for players to go to some lengths to hide their bases and loot, whether through putting them in obscure locations, building complex traps and other deterrents or (our favorite method) through tricks such as fake bases.

Of the many styles of fake base we've seen, none is so effective as the awesome and fun-to-build Double Bluff Base. The premise is simple: build a fake base that is actually an entrance to your real base. This method is highly effective for two reasons: 1) Players looking for your base will get excited, and then quickly disappointed and bored when they realize it's a "fake" base. Few will ever come back, and if they mess it up or take stuff, it doesn't matter because it will mostly be filled with cheap stuff. And 2) You can move in and out of this area without people wondering what's up, as they'll think you're just improving your fake base.

A small house like this against a hill and covered by Trees is a perfect fake base.

The fake base works by building a small structure that has a method for opening an entrance to a larger one that is hidden behind or underneath the smaller "fake" base. The three main components of making this build successful are:

- Making the fake base detailed enough to trick people

- Hiding the larger structure as well as possible

- Building an entrance to the real base that is hard to notice and to open

When it comes to the fake base, what you want is to imagine what would draw you in if you thought you were close to another player's real base, and then what would frustrate you and make you leave. So, for instance, you don't want the fake base to be too easy to find (so don't put giant glowing towers or the like), but you don't want to entirely hide it either. Make it so that there's one direction that part of it can be pretty easily seen from or

An example AND Gate hooked up to our secret door in this false hill. Of course, for yours you want to put your switches farther away from each other and hide all of the Redstone underground.

something similar. Inside, you want it to look real when a player approaches (so looks real from the outside, can see things like a few Chests, etc. inside it from the outside), but when a player actually enters, it shouldn't take them long to realize it's fake, as there shouldn't be much more inside.

Make this bluff even more effective by adding a few simple traps (like Pressure Plates attached to Arrow shooting Dispensers) and maybe even some signage that indicates the base is fake ("Haha, got you sucker!" or that kind of thing). For the fake loot Chests, fill them with something annoying like Gravel, and your intruders should take off pretty quickly.

Your real base should be in a mountain or hill directly behind the fake one, or buried underneath it. Remember: this is your secret base, so keeping it completely hidden and as safe as possible is paramount (don't go adding windows or easy-to-see Doors or the like on the outside). Make it so that if a player were to walk by or over it, they wouldn't notice anything different from a normal area and will think that there is just natural landscape around them.

One good idea is to put at least four or five layers of block between your base and your fake base by creating a tunnel or hallway after the secret door. Invaders of your fake base will often punch out the ground to see if there's anything below, so trick them further by making it seem like there isn't.

Screenshot: Minecraft® ™ & © 2009–2013 Mojang/Notch.

A view of the Sticky Pistons that drive the secret door.

Another trick for keeping your base safe and concealed is to build an outer shell (around your base but still underground or inside a mountain so it can't be seen) of Obsidian or Lava. That way if a player does dig down and hit your base, all they see is a wall of tough-to-get-through Obsidian or Lava. Usually, they'll just turn back, and if they don't, they will probably have a very hard time getting in.

The final touch, and the most important for your secret base is, of course, your secret door. There are many, many methods and strategies for doing this, and you can come up with your own if you like, but ours involves using an AND Gate (see the Advanced Inventions section) with two hidden Levers that, when flipped at the same time, cause two Sticky Pistons attached to two blocks to slide back, revealing the door to your true base.

Build the secret door into your floor or a wall, attaching blocks of the surrounding natural material (Stone or Dirt usually) that is in the area. Hide your Sticky Pistons and Redstone behind more blocks of the same material or underground, and run the Redstone through a hidden AND Gate (you'll probably need some Repeaters to stretch the signal), and then to two Levers. Place one Lever in your fake base (have it function to do something else as well, like open a Door, for another layer of trickery) and one Lever someplace else, preferably out of sight and well-hidden. This way someone can come in and flip the Lever in your base and not open the secret door unless you have already flipped the second Lever, making your base secure.

Building into Natural Structures

This is less of a specific build and more of a fun concept: why not let nature do the design for you and just build into a mountain or cliffside? Minecraft's environment-constructing algorithms are pretty awesome at times, as anyone who has come around a corner and gone "Whoa" when they saw what was there knows. Make that "natural" beauty your own and incorporate a home into it. Having to work within and around the shape that's already there, and building by removing blocks instead of adding (for the most part), can spark the imagination and get a builder thinking differently, and it makes for some neat builds.

View of a lake from a cliff? We say yes to that.

This is what the tool at Plotz.co.uk looks like showing you how to build a layer of a sphere.

Structure Tools

Planning out big structures can be hard, and planning out giant, symmetrical structures like domes? Well that takes a seriously organized mind to get right without help. Lucky for us non-math geniuses, there are actually some really cool tools online to help you plan out your build, and they're free!

There are basically two types of main tools out there right now: plotting tools that allow you to draw out plans for a whole build, and math-based tools that show you layer-by-layer how to build complex structures like orbs and domes.

MineDraft lets you plan out your builds vertically or horizontally.

In the first category, check out **MineDraft.net.** This straightforward site simply gives you a grid on which to place representations of the various blocks and items in the game. Click on the block you'd like, put it where you want on the grid, and continue until you've got a map of your next build. Especially great for working out Redstone circuits, this tool is a tremendous help for complex builds.

For the more math-based tools, Plotz.co.uk is king of the spheres. What we mean by that is that it's a site that helps you build spheres and domes of various sizes by showing you what to build layer by layer. Instead of having to keep the entire, giant dome in mind while counting the blocks, so it ends up even and nice-looking, Plotz does it for you, and you simply have to recreate what you see on the screen. Your domes will never look so crisp and perfect!

Plotz also shows you how to build a few random structures, like this observatory.

Screenshot: Minecraft® ™ & © 2009–2013 Mojang/Notch.

What To Do When

There's a moment in just about every long-haul Crafting session where you come up against something tough, and you're just not sure what to do about it. Minecraft is full of these kind of moments, whether it's deciding to stay down in your mine for another fifteen minutes before heading back to base, or whether you suddenly find yourself in peril and aren't sure if you should fight, fly or just throw in the towel and reload from your last save. While there are really no wrong answers in this game that's all about experimentation and playing how you like, there are some tips for certain situations that we can give you that can make your next mining trip go a bit smoother (by which we mean less full of death and woe).

1. You're lost and can't find home (or anything else you recognize).

We all love the goofy, blocky graphics of Minecraft, but we also have to admit that they can make it hard to keep your sense of direction. Since there are only so many types of blocks and environments, you can quickly get turned around both above and below ground. If you're stuck out in the wild and are starting to think you'll never see home again, try these tips.

- Get up high. If you're above ground, create a dirt tower so you can look out over a bigger area, or climb a tree. If you're underground, stop trying to find your way out naturally and just dig up in a staircase pattern. Moving up is almost always beneficial in Minecraft when lost or stuck, and you can always go back down if you need to!

- Mark your path. Always, always mark your path, especially when you're already lost. Use towers, torches, just about anything you'll recognize, and you'll start to weed out all the wrong directions (and will stop going in circles, as can definitely happen).

- Use the Cobblestone/Nether Rack "north" trick. If you look at blocks of either of these, you'll see that they have an "L" shape on the texture (on the regular texture pack). If you situate your miner so that the L is facing the correct direction (meaning it looks like the letter should), you are facing north.

Screenshot: Minecraft® ™ & © 2009–2013 Mojang/Notch.

2. You're stuck outside/underground without resources and mobs are about.

Mobs don't care if you're ready for combat or not: they're coming for you. It's pretty likely that you're gonna find yourself in a bad spot at some point, with mobs a'comin' and no Sword, Bow or other weapons to speak of. What do you do?

- Get up high. Like with being lost, getting off the ground level is an excellent combat measure. Mobs have a hard time climbing even one block and most cant climb two (just Spiders), so put some air between you and your foes.

- Run straight through. Sometimes the best way to survive is to just put on a burst of speed and try and break through the line of mobs. If possible, eat something before you do this.

- Protect your resources. It's always easier to come back and find a Chest with items in it than it is to rush back to get the gear that dropped when you died. Bring Chests with you when you mine and store all of your important stuff when in a bad spot before trying to escape.

- If possible, build a mini-mini murder fort. Obviously you don't have time to do any major construction, but if you can surround yourself with blocks and leave just a little space to attack through, you should be able to time it so that you can hit mobs and they can't reach you. Very effective in a pinch.

3. There's a Creeper in your home (or project, or mine, etc.).

It happens, sometimes a lot, and it's terrifying. There's one thing to do.

- Get out. Immediately. It's the Creeper's home now. Okay, not really to that last bit, but seriously, just go. While you might be able to kill the thing, there's just too much at risk. Unless you don't care what happens to the place, it's always better to leave and let the creepy thing see itself out or despawn than it is to risk having to put half your house back together.

4. A Creeper done blew up your home.

But of course, sometimes you just can't get away in time. Creepers do be creepin'. But don't panic; you have options.

- Consider reloading. It may seem cheap, but so is showing up unannounced, sneaking right next to you and your beloved project and blowing it to smithereens. If you saved less than five minutes ago or if rebuilding would take more time than re-doing what you've been doing, you might want to reload.

- Take the opportunity to make it better. We all get distracted by new projects and tend to leave old ones sitting for a long time. It's super common to jump in someone's world and see that their bedroom is a lot shabbier than whatever the newest project they're workin' on is, as miners often get so caught up in other stuff that they don't take the time to update or upgrade their older work. If a Creeper knocks a hole in your house, well maybe it's time to add that moat you've always wanted! This is one of the greatest things about Minecraft: when things get destroyed, it gives you the chance to make it better!

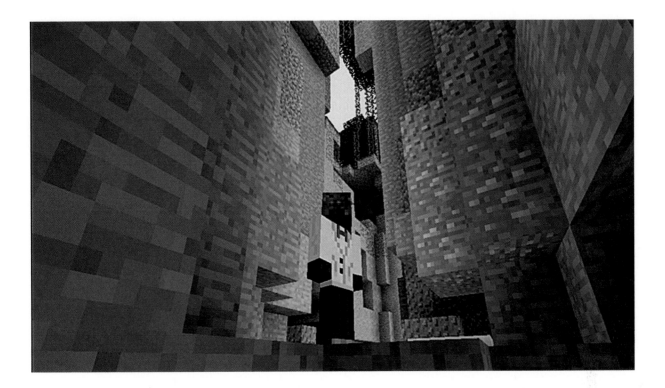

5. You fell in a pit/cave/ravine without torches.

Falling into darkness is hard and a bit nerve-wracking; it usually starts with a bit of panic as you wonder how you can possibly get out without light. But...

- Just dig forward and up. Hopefully you have tools, but either way, just put a block in front of you (you can always kinda just a bit, even in the dark) and break it. Then point up and break the one above it, and then the one behind that. Jump up and repeat. You will eventually either A) find light, B) get out or C) crack into another drop and fall more, possibly to your death. Whatever happens, you'll at least get out.

Screenshot: Minecraft® ™ & © 2009–2013 Mojang/Notch.

6. You have a bunch of resources and wonder if it's time to go back, but aren't sure if you want to yet.

Oh the many, many times we've thought to ourselves "I should find a Chest, but I'll just explore this one more cave." There's an answer:

- Don't stay out. If you're wondering if you should head to a Chest, the answer is almost always yes. Think of it like this: you just did a bunch of work, you have some good stuff, and you are currently safe, healthy and you know the way back. These are things you know for sure, right now. Give Minecraft the chance, and it will change one or all of those things within seconds. Err on the side of caution (and keeping your loot).

- Or, build a chest here and now and drop yer goods. You can always come back in a few minutes and grab it all, and at least you know it'll be safe.

- Or, save the game. Don't be afraid to use the save feature to your advantage. Hit pause and save real quick, that way you can load from right there and make a better decision if things go south.

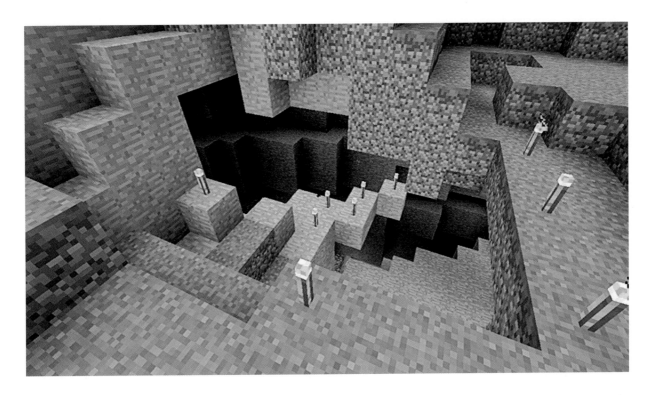

7. You find somethin' awesome, but you aren't geared/prepared/ready to jump into it.

Abandoned Mineshafts are one of the more dangerous structures in the game. Don't go in unless you're ready.

Cool things are around almost every corner, and you'll end up stumbling across a ton of them while you were on your way elsewhere.

- Don't overreach. Taking a peek is fine, but if you don't think you're prepped for a big cave encounter, **don't go down the big, dark, dangerous cave.**

- Mark it well. Light the place up with Torches, build a big tower of Dirt, make a Flower path back home or better yet bust out a Map and write down the coordinates. Just because you aren't ready to go now doesn't mean you should let neat places and valuable areas be forgotten. Make it so you'll definitely be able to find it again, and then do.

8. A structure or area is giving you trouble because it is getting too complex and dangerous.

In most games, you're pretty much stuck with having to navigate complex areas as they are, but this is Minecraft. We have better ways of dealing with nests of enemies, such as...

• Take the area apart. Just start simplifying the area by removing blocks and making it into one big room. You don't have to play fair; mobs certainly don't. Turn that confusing cave system or dangerous mineshaft into *your* area. Eliminate the threat by controlling the land, and you'll find that Fortresses and the like are just oh so much less intimidating.

9. Something interesting pops up while you're in the middle of a project.

Say you're carving out a base, and you stumble across the entrance to a cave or a big deposit of ore. What do you do? Abandon your project and deal with this now, or save it for later?

- If it's ore, go for it. Get ore until there is no more, and then fill in the area so it is just Cobblestone. Your later projects will thank you, and you won't lose the organization of what you were working on.

- If it's a structure or system, secure the area, mark it, and come back later. There is nothing more dangerous than leaving an entrance to an open cave or structure in your base or project, because you never know what can come sneaking up out of the depths all the way through your home and even to your bedroom. Where there's dark, there's danger. Control the situation first, finish what you were working on, then come back and dominate that structure and whatever foolish mobs dare to dwell in it.

10. You can't find what you're looking for.

Sometimes you start a game and crack straight into a Diamond-filled ravine/Fortress, and sometimes you go weeks on a world without seeing either. While it's never guaranteed to find anything in the game, there is a system that can help.

- Use the Staircase Down, Ladder Up method. Seriously guys, this method works wonders. All you do is create a staircase down to the Bedrock and when you're at the bottom, build a Ladder that goes all the way to the surface from there. Create a few of these in different directions and on different parts of the map, and you end up covering an enormous area in very efficient manner. You'll find ore, you'll find structures, you'll find mobs; you'll find just about everything. Even more effective when combined with tunnels, branch mining and clearing out levels around the staircase.

Beating the Game

Where You Should Be in Your Game

Most games of Minecraft that actually reach The End happen one of two ways: either the players collect the needed items as they otherwise play and get the opportunity naturally (which takes a very long time), or they specifically set out at some point to collect what they need to get to The End and make it a goal. It really isn't likely that you can play casually and even get to The End, and even if you do, you are even less likely to do well there, as it is arguably the toughest scenario in the entire game.

You'll need the best gear you can get to beat Minecraft.

Because of this, your game should be fairly well along before you attempt The End. Check off as many items as possible from the following list before you make your trip, and your chances at success will multiply.

You Need

- Diamond gear (as much as possible)
- Lots of Obsidian (meaning more Diamonds needed in order to make Pickaxes)
- The ability to enchant (requires Diamonds, Obsidian and a Book to make an Enchantment Table)
- Potions (requires a Blaze Rod for a Brewing Stand)

As Diamonds are the hardest ore to find in the game, and two of the other three items on this list require Diamond (and the last a Blaze Rod, even harder to find), you'll need to either set out to find Diamonds early in the game, or be at a point where you've collected quite a bit already before you can think about going to The End.

Part 1: Getting to the Nether

One of the primary ingredients for getting to The End is the Blaze Rod, which drops when Blazes are killed in the Nether. Naturally then, getting to the Nether is your first goal, and of course, this means you need a Nether Portal.

Ye Olde Nether Portal, ready to go.

There are two ways to create a Nether Portal: either mine Obsidian and create the Nether Portal shape (Obsidian surrounding an empty space that's two blocks wide and three tall), or use Water poured over Lava that is in the correct shape to create the Portal. The first method takes Diamond, but a lot less finagling with Lava, while the second lets you skip the Diamond. We suggest going the longer, Diamond-using route however, as the benefits of collecting a lot of Diamond will help you out later.

Screenshot: Minecraft® ™ & © 2009–2013 Mojang/Notch.

Nether Forts can look like this when they spawn over Lava. Look for bridges and towers.

Part 2: The Nether

Once in the Nether, you need to create a safe area that you can base out of. Though you can't place Beds in the Nether (they will simply explode), you can bring building materials. Cobblestone is resistant to Ghast explosions, as is Obsidian, so using one or both of those materials to create a little base is an excellent idea. It's also prudent to take decent armor and weapons along, at the very least bringing some Iron gear if you can't go all the way for Diamond.

When you're set up with a safe place, you need to start looking around for Nether Forts. This can be a bit tricky, as your spawn point in the Nether can often be underground, requiring you to dig a while. However, if you find a pretty big room, especially one with a giant Lava pool at the bottom, you've probably found an area with a Nether Fort in it. The Nether is much smaller than the overworld, so if you don't see a Fort close around your base, you should try digging straight, skinny tunnels until you find one. Another option is to create a second Nether Portal in the overworld in a different spot, as this will spawn you elsewhere in the Nether.

The Blaze spawner in action, plus a random Magma Cube.

When you find a Nether Fort, look for Blaze spawners. These are usually on little Nether Brick platforms at the end of bridges in Nether Forts, and you can see them pretty easily due to all the yellow Blaze flying around.

Killing Blazes is tricky. You want good gear, preferably some Golden Apples to resist the Blaze's fire attack, some Snowballs and some blocks to build with. Blazes can fly and shoot at you from a distance, so use the blocks to contain the area around the spawner, making it so they can't get out of your range. Snowballs do 3 damage to Blazes and are cheap and easy to throw, so they can be your best weapon against these fiery foes. Use those, Bows and Arrows and the best Sword and Armor you can make, and you should be okay.

When you find the End Portal room, you'll need to deal with this Silverfish spawner first.

Part 3: Opening the End Gate

To open the End Gate, you need to collect a certain amount of items and then find the gate. On the collection side, your first object is to get at least 9 Blaze Rods. One Blaze Rod makes two Blaze Powders, and one Blaze Powder plus one Ender Pearl makes one Eye of Ender. End Portals require 12 Eyes of Ender to open (at the maximum, some already have a few in them), and you'll need a few more in order to actually find the Portal. Additionally, you'll want an Enchantment Table, which takes another Blaze Rod. Add all of that together, and you need at least 9 Blaze Rods.

We've already shown you how to kill Blazes for Blaze Rods above, but you'll also need the Ender Pearls as well, which you get from killing Endermen. This is when the Kill More Mobs section of this guide will come in handy, and you'll probably have to kill quite a few as they don't always drop the Pearls. You should collect at least 16 Ender Pearls, and 20 is even safer.

Give your Portal base everything you can, especially a Bed. You'll probably be dying a few times, so you'll be back here soon.

Once you have your Rods and have made them into Powder (leaving one for your Enchantment Table) and have combined the Powder with the Pearls to make Eyes of Ender, you need to find a Stronghold. This is where your extra Eyes come into play: throw your Eyes of Ender, and they will shoot out toward a Stronghold. You may be able to pick up the Eye again, but they can also break so be careful about not throwing too many (make sure you keep at least 12).

Follow the Eyes, and eventually you'll get to a Stronghold. You'll have to explore the Stronghold, but somewhere in it you will find a room with Lava, a Nether Portal and some Silverfish blocks. Make sure to kill and contain the Silverfish, then build a containment area/mini-base around the Portal. Finally, activate it by placing the Eyes of Ender into the Portal blocks, and you'll see it kick on!

Screenshot: Minecraft® ™ & © 2009–2013 Mojang/Notch.

Part 4: Prep

Now hold yer horses young Crafter: you need to get ready before you dive through that Portal. Besides getting all the best gear you can, you also need to do a few more things before you make the plunge.

- Get the area around your Portal ready. If you die in The End, you just go back to your spawn point in the overworld. Make that mini-base around your Portal and include a Bed that you've slept in and Chests with tons of gear in them. This way when you die, you just gear up again and head right back to The End.

- Take the best gear, and enchant as much of it as is possible.

- In addition to a Diamond Sword or so, bring a Bow and as many Arrows as you can.

- Also bring Potions, a Pumpkin (to wear if the Endermen bother you too much), Water Buckets (to scare off the Endermen), Obsidian, Ladders, Chests and food. This is your kit to beat The End.

Once you've got your base prepared and have everything you need, you're ready to go wreck you an Ender Dragon. Whoo!

Part 5: Dealing with The End

Build a little fort of Obsidian like this in order to survive your attack on the Dragon.

You'll notice right off the bat that The End is different from the other areas. First thing's first: you need to get off the little area you're floating on and over to the main island. Use Obsidian to build a bridge over, and be careful! The main island is covered in Endermen, not to mention that big ole Ender Dragon flying around.

You can always go straight to the attack, but this isn't likely to get you anywhere but dead unless you are just insanely geared up and good at combat. The best bet for survival and success is, as we so often say in Minecrafter, to control the area.

Use your Obsidian to build yourself a small fort or safe area in The End. Make this so that Endermen can't get in and the Ender Dragon can't see you (so you'll need to make a few layers within it, or some entrance passageways that twist and are too small for the Endermen to get through). The Dragon can't break Obsidian, so you'll be relatively safe to put down resupply Chests in your Obsidian fort, as well as to use it to shoot at your enemies.

Endermen are mostly just pests in The End, so it's best just to kill them quickly or avoid them altogether. Use your Buckets of Water and Pumpkin for this (Endermen won't see you with a Pumpkin on your head, and they hate and are damaged by Water).

Screenshot: Minecraft® ™ & © 2009–2013 Mojang/Notch.

Shoot these crystal, Dragon-charger things with arrows if possible, as they explode.

Part 6: Killing the Ender Dragon

Building an Obsidian fort and messin' with Endermen is pretty fun, but you're here for one reason: to kill that big darn Dragon. You'll notice that beams are flying out of those giant Obsidian pillars and touching the Dragon as he flies around: these come out of crystals on the tops of the pillars, and they heal the Dragon. You can't kill him with these still going, as he'll just heal, so you need to take them out.

There are two common methods for this: shoot out the crystals from below with a Bow or Snowballs, or climb the pillars and break the crystals with a Sword. Either method works, though you'll have to be a good shot for the first, and you'll have to deal with the crystals exploding when broken for the second.

Once the crystals are out, attack the Dragon. Enchanted Bows are probably the best weapon here, as you can hit the Dragon when flying, but you can use just about any combat method you want. The keys here are these: have a big supply of the best gear you can get, avoid the fire blasts (they're pretty slow), hide when you need to (in fact, staying in your base and shooting out of it is a great method), and use items like food and potions to keep your health and strength up constantly.

A crystal shatters from a bow shot.

It will be expensive, you will die a lot, and it will take a long time. But when you finally see that health bar drop to nil, and the Dragon starts exploding light everywhere and dropping the craziest amount of experience you've ever seen, you'll know it was all worth it. You've just "beat" Minecraft, brave young Crafter!

Note: Make sure to read the infamous "End Poem" after killing the Ender Dragon. It's a very cool piece of writing, and it'll make you see the game in a different light! It's also one of the only actual "story" parts in the game, so be sure not to miss it.

Screenshot: Minecraft® ™ & © 2009–2013 Mojang/Notch.